I've known Bob and Loretta Yandian for three decades. We've ministered together many times overseas as well in the States. Bob is a valuable member of my Board of Directors and ministers regularly in our Charis Bible College. We've spent vacations together many times.

Bob has not only ministered powerfully into my life, but I've seen firsthand the Lord use Bob to transform those in our meetings with signs and wonders following. And Bob lives what he preaches. Bob and Loretta are proven ministers. They've weathered many storms in ministry as well as their personal lives with the same faith they preach. This isn't theory to them but something that is working in their lives.

Bob has been ministering grace ever since I've known him and his revelation on God's grace will be invaluable in you receiving your healing. Faith works by love which is God's grace in action. You need this truth. These truths will set you free.

ANDREW WOMMACK
President of Andrew Wommack Ministries
Founder and President of Charis Bible College

The Grace of Healing

The Grace of Healing

of Healing

Revealing God's Heart to Heal

BOB YANDIAN

Published by Harrison House Publishers
Shippensburg, PA 17257

Cover design by Eileen Rockwell
Interior design by Terry Clifton

ISBN 13 TP: 978-1-6803-1504-2
ISBN 13 eBook: 978-1-6803-1505-9
ISBN 13 HC: 978-1-6803-1507-3
ISBN 13 LP: 978-1-6803-1506-6

For Worldwide Distribution, Printed in the U.S.A.
3 4 5 6 7 8 / 24 23 22

Contents

Foreword

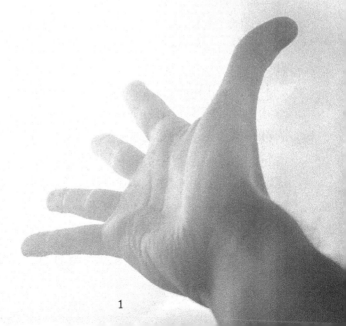

If you are like most believers, the subject of healing is very important to you. It is likely you've received healing at some time in your life, or at some point, you've been disappointed because healing didn't come as quickly as you wished. Many people have questions about healing—why it comes to some, why it doesn't come to others, and what the Bible authoritatively teaches on this important subject that touches all of our lives, etc. Well, Bob Yandian's book *The Grace of Healing* will answer many of these questions!

The Grace of Healing is pure Bob Yandian: *Bible-based, practical, straight to the point, and no nonsense.* What Bob has written in these pages on grace and faith—and how these divine elements cooperate and work together for physical healing—is without question the most helpful and practical material on the subject that I have ever read. In fact, I was so enthralled by the material in this book that I read it from cover to cover in one sitting.

In his writings, Pastor Bob brilliantly mixes the roles of grace and faith. Today grace is emphasized by many teachers, which is good, but Bob reminds us that every act of grace must be received by faith. While others have masterfully taught on the subject of faith, I've never read anything that makes faith easier to understand than what is written in *The Grace of Healing*. As a reader, you will see that every point in this wonderful book is absolutely clear, easy to understand, and readily applicable to your life. It is brilliantly written and enjoyably honest.

As one who has given most of my life to the study of the Greek New Testament, I can say that much has been said about the Greek word *sozo* (the Greek word for *salvation*) by numerous teachers over the years. But in the pages you are about to read, Pastor Bob accurately deals with the many, various uses of this word in the New Testament and categorically shows that it not only includes *eternal salvation*, but also *healing* and *deliverance* for our lives right now.

In chapter two, Pastor Bob writes about Jesus as our Passover Lamb, and what he has penned about this truth is simply powerful. What he has written about the value of the bowl of Jesus' blood poured out for you and me cannot be overstated. As the pages continue, Bob shows that from the very beginning, God has placed healing inside nature and inside every human being and has provided everything—along with supernatural power—to bring His people into a state of health.

Today the world spends billions of dollars annually on special foods, diets, and exercise programs. Regardless, many people remain physically sick. Pastor Bob hilariously deals with the issues of diet and the role of exercise and then superbly explains the difference between health and fitness in a way that I had never thought of before. You will find this approach to be refreshing, practical, full of common sense, and so enjoyable. In fact, if that chapter of the book affects you as it did me, you will find yourself laughing out loud because you'll be able to relate so easily to everything he has written. As a reader hungry for truth, you will devour the pages in which Bob enumerates the things that contribute to health besides diet—*elements that may affect your long-term health more than what you eat!*

As a leader who has counseled and prayed for many who were sick, I am aware that people frequently think certain physical conditions are more challenging for God to heal—or that many have thought they may have done something to cause their sickness, thus making their condition more difficult to be healed. Pastor

Bob demolishes those arguments forever. He shows that even if you're sick from behaviors that made you sick, it does not change the fact that God has healing for you if you'll take it by grace and faith. Anyone in need of healing will be enthralled by reading the chapter on God's graciousness to restore every person's health regardless of the individual's own contribution to his or her medical or physical condition.

As Pastor Bob says, "There is no disease God will not heal, including the ones that are our fault." In pure Bob Yandian style, he dismantles religious thinking and sets every reader on the path to healing and wholeness. This part of the book is so liberating—I laughed with a thankful heart when I read it.

Furthermore, Bob Yandian proves out the fact that Jesus is the same yesterday, today, and forever. What Jesus did 2,000 years ago is exactly what He *is* doing today and *will be* doing tomorrow. Since Jesus healed even the most severe medical cases known to man, He is still doing that very thing today. You will discover that it doesn't matter what you're trying to overcome physically, Jesus paid the price for that condition to be healed and for you to be delivered from it. He is ready right now to release His power to heal you.

I could continue on and on about how deeply this book impacted me. The pages about Jesus' sacrificial death and about Jesus as our Jubilee will melt you with thankfulness and a greater revelation of the love of God. But a particularly special blessing to me was what Pastor Bob wrote about Communion—about how God's healing power can be activated in us when we receive the elements of Communion by faith. That section of this book is so impacting that I intend to implement much of that teaching in my own ministry.

No one teaches on this subject like Pastor Bob Yandian, and in *The Grace of Healing*, he really knocks it out of the ballpark. I *love* this book! As a matter of fact, I can confidently say that *The Grace of Healing* is among the best books I've EVER read on the subject of faith and grace in the context of healing. I am certain that in these pages, you will discover how healing can be practically received into your own life.

Everyone will benefit from reading these pages. So, Pastor Bob, thank you for what you have written in this ever-useful book and for walking us into these truths in such an enjoyable, practical, and tangible way. Wow...after writing this foreword, I feel like I'm ready to reread *The Grace of Healing* again right now!

RICK RENNER

Author, Teacher, Pastor, Broadcaster

Rick Renner Ministries and

Moscow Good News Church

Tulsa, Oklahoma, and Moscow, Russia

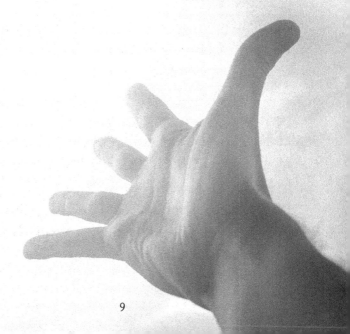

Introduction

I was not raised in a denomination but in a Pentecostal fellowship of churches, all united by a belief in the grace of God. In fact, we were called Pentecostal Grace. While many today are coming into a knowledge of the grace of God, I was raised understanding the greatness of God's grace and mercy accompanied by an understanding of the infilling of the Holy Spirit and the operation of His supernatural gifts. We were unique among other Pentecostal churches, who all had a common belief that God's grace remaining in your life was determined by your conduct. Our small group of churches even believed in eternal security or once saved always saved. And we would certainly fight you if you did not believe in that doctrine.

Although we believed that salvation came by grace and through faith only, we did not believe the same regarding the infilling of the Holy Spirit or divine healing. We would pray for people to be filled with the Holy Spirit, but they had to "tarry" or wait, at times for hours, for His presence to fill the room and people's lives. We would pray for the sick to be healed, but we believed it was more of the sovereign will of God as to who would be healed and who would not. We thought this was grace. As I grew up, I was greatly confused with the difference between God's grace and His sovereignty. Grace never was designed to be hopefully waited for, but to be immediately received.

Grace never was designed to be hopefully waited for, but to be immediately received.

Which brings me to the other half of the life of a Christian: the walk of faith. In my junior year of college, the Lord spoke to me that I was to be a teacher of the Word of God. I began to bring as many books to my dorm room as I could take from my father's library. They were all on grace, and I grew more and more in the wonderful message of God's mercy and love. I went to a Bible college in Tulsa the next year and was married to Loretta at the semester break. Nothing opened up for me to use my calling, so I taught Sunday school classes at my church and worked a secular job to pay the bills.

After two years of marriage, a job opened up for me producing cassette tapes (remember them?) and a radio broadcast for Kenneth E. Hagin, a Bible teacher of faith who is now in heaven. To produce a tape for the public, I had to listen to the message, edit for content and time, and make the master. I listened to each message three times. Finally, the understanding of faith dawned on me and a new phase of spiritual life took off for Loretta and me. I taught at Kenneth Hagin's RHEMA Bible Training Center for four years, and during the last year. I become the dean of instructors.

After a total of seven years working for Kenneth Hagin Ministries, I was called to pastor the church Loretta and I had been attending since its beginning, seven years before. I pastored for thirty-three years and saw miraculous growth in attendance and in the spiritual lives of the people. I owe much gratitude to the authors of the books I read, the teaching ministry of my father, Kenneth Hagin and other ministers, and many pastors who spoke into my life. With so many things to thank God for, I think my life's successes could be easily attributed to two things designed by God to work together: His grace and my faith.

I realize both these doctrines of grace and faith have been taken to extreme through the years. Many on the side of grace deny the need for faith, and many on the side of faith deny the need for God's grace. But balancing the two brings the believer into the true joy God intended. For those who only see a need for grace, the Christian life, as well as healing, become a matter of God's sovereignty. In other words, God saves and heals those He chooses, and a person's faith has little or nothing to do with it. For those who only see a need for faith, life becomes legalistic. Salvation, healing, and the Christian life become works, a struggle to obtain and to maintain.

In this book I plan to speak on two works of the cross—salvation and divine healing. Both come from God's grace, and both are received by faith. More time will be given to healing since most of us already understand that God's plan for salvation comes from grace. It is healing many Christians do not fully understand, never attributing this power which comes from God as also, like the new birth, originating from His grace.

My trust is that many of you will finally see the physical change you have been waiting for when you find the missing ingredient and understand the grace of healing.

BOB YANDIAN

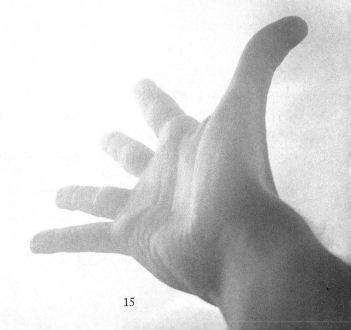

Chapter 1

Two Words That Say It All

Grace and Faith

For by grace you have been saved through faith, and that [faith] *not of yourselves; it is the gift of God, not of works, lest anyone should boast* (Ephesians 2:8-9) (Author comments bracketed).

The two words that say it all are *grace* and *faith*. If you will notice in this well-known verse of scripture, *grace comes before faith*. Grace is God's hand reaching out to you filled with *"...all the things that pertain to life and godliness..."* (2 Peter 1:3). Faith is our empty hand reaching out to receive what God is giving us in grace. Faith only receives what God gives in grace. Grace is the major part, the hard part, and God's part. God is responsible for grace. Faith is the minor part, the easy part, and our part. God leaves the easy part to us.

Givers and Takers

Grace must come before faith. Otherwise, we would have nothing to receive. We cannot manufacturer one thing for our salvation or spiritual life afterward. Only God can create our salvation, healing, or the meeting of any of our needs. God does the impossible thing. All we do with faith is receive what God creates and generously offers to us. God is the Giver, and we are the takers. But God's giving has to come before our taking.

Faith only receives what God gives in grace.

Also notice in our text verse, that even our faith is a gift of God's grace (see also Acts 3:16). Not only does God offer what we have need of, but He even gives us the ability to receive it. I owe everything to God and His grace. No wonder the rest of the verse says *"...lest anyone should boast"* (Ephesians 2:9). Knowing God gives us everything and then gives us the ability to receive it, leaves no room at all for us to boast.

Would You Like A Free Ferrari?

Suppose I came to your church to speak and asked for you, by name, to come to the front because I had a gift for you. I then tell you, "I know you have always wanted a new red Ferrari, so I went by the dealership before I came to your church and picked up one for you. It's waiting in a semi from Ferrari outside the church. Here's the key, all you have to do is take it from my hand."

Your first words would probably be, "But wait! I can't afford the car. I know it costs over $250,000."

"No, I already paid for it," I explain. "You owe nothing. Just take the key!"

"But I can't afford the insurance for the car. It will cost more than I paid for my present car."

"No, I've also arranged to pay for the insurance for the car for the rest of your life. You will always be covered. Just take the key!"

You still resist. "What about when the warranty is over? I can't afford the brake rotors on that car."

"No, I've purchased a maintenance plan for the car for the rest of your life. Just take the key!"

"But what kind of mileage does it get?"

"Terrible! But I am also giving you a credit card that will pay for the fuel for the rest of your life. Just take the key!"

"But I feel like I should give you something for the car."

"Don't insult my generosity. I paid for the car; you can't even pay the tip. Just take the key!"

You then would be *stupid* not to take the key. Everything has been covered. The only effort you must put into this whole transaction is to reach out and take the key.

Suppose as soon as church was over, a reporter from the local TV station met you at the back door as you were leaving to drive your new car home. He says he heard about the free gift and wanted to do an interview with you.

"Would you tell us how you feel about a new free Ferrari?" he asks.

"You should have seen me reach out and take the key," you say. "My arms glistened in the light of the auditorium, and my muscles bulged as I took the key fob and slowly wrapped each finger around it. *You should have seen me!*"

The reporter might ask, "Yes, but what about the man who bought the car for you, paid for the insurance, maintenance, and gas? Doesn't he deserve the credit?"

In the same way, that's how wrong it is to brag on your faith. All the glory should go to God for His grace. Your faith only received what God made and planned for you to have from the foundation of the world. He brought His Son into the world to die for you, take your curse, sin and sickness, defeat it, and be raised from the dead to offer you the gift of eternal life and all other benefits in this life. That's even better than a Ferrari! A car is temporary, but God's gifts are eternal.

Since our faith is also a gift from God, it leaves no room at all for boasting. We have nothing to brag about. God receives all the thanks and glory.

A Word for Salvation That Says It All

Just like the Ferrari included insurance, maintenance, and fuel, so does God's gift of salvation include all the extra benefits so we can fully enjoy our eternal life. Healing and the blessings of life are also included with the new birth.

"For by grace are you saved through faith..." (Ephesians 2:8). The Greek word for *saved* is sōzō. *The Scofield Reference Bible* in Romans 1:16 calls this word *sōzō* "the great inclusive word of the Gospel." It has up to seven different uses in the gospels and epistles. Let me give you some of its meanings from Strong's concordance, *The Exhaustive Concordance of the Bible*, entry 4982: "To save, deliver, make whole, preserve safe from danger, loss, destruction. *Sōzō* occurs fifty-four times in the Gospels (not counting Luke 17:33 where it is *zōogonḗsei,* "to rescue from death"). Of the instances where *sōzō* is used, fourteen relate to deliverance from disease or demon possession. In twenty instances, the inference is to the rescue of physical life from some impending peril or instant death. The remaining twenty times, the reference is to spiritual salvation."

Let's put some of these definitions into our passage. For by grace are you saved from your sins through faith. You are saved from peril and death through faith.

And, you also are saved from demons and sickness through faith.

Let's also put some of these definitions into a verse we are all familiar with—Jesus' healing of the woman with the issue of blood: *"He said to her, 'Daughter, thy faith hath made thee whole* [sṓzō]*...'"* (Mark 5:34 KJV) (Author comments bracketed).

When we are saved, our sins are completely forgiven and removed—every one of them. So it is when we receive healing.

When we are saved, our sins are completely forgiven and removed—every one of them. So it is when we receive healing. We are not just partially healed but made completely whole of the infirmity. This woman had no trace of the sickness left in her blood. She simply reached out with her faith and took her healing:

"...*thy faith has made you whole.*" This sounds a lot like *sōzō* in Ephesians 2:8, "*For by grace you have been saved* [healed and made whole] *through faith...*" (Author comments bracketed).

The last half of the word *sōzō* is from the Greek word *zoe*, or *life* (*zoology* is from this word, meaning "the study of life"). Strong's definition also adds, "*Sōzō* involves the preservation of life, either physical or spiritual." Our faith gives supernatural quickening to a sinful life, a poverty-ridden life, and a life of sickness and disease.

A Word for Faith That Says It All

God's grace has given to us through Jesus' resurrection power "...*all things that pertain unto life and godliness...*" (2 Peter 1:3). Whatever you need for your spiritual or natural life is in God's hand, and all that is involved on your part is to take it. God's hand holds all the grace heaven has to offer. Your hand simply *receives* it. The key word here is *receive*.

> *But as many as received Him, to them He gave*
> *the right to become children of God, to those who*
> *believe in His name* (John 1:12).

In the hand of the Lord Jesus is eternal life and the power to grow into full grown sons and daughters of God. All that is needed from us is to *receive* it. But what else is in the hand of Jesus just waiting to be received?

> *The blind receive their sight, and the lame walk,*
> *the lepers are cleansed, and the deaf hear, the*
> *dead are raised up, and the poor have the gospel*
> *preached to them* (Matthew 11:5 KJV).

As well as the gospel being preached to the sinner, healing also is offered for the "receiving" to the blind, lame, leprous, deaf, dead, and God's prosperity is offered to the poor. That truly is everything we need for life and godliness, all found in the hand of God. Why do you doubt the Scriptures telling you what God has already prepared for you? What do you need from the Lord? It is in His hand of grace reaching out to you right now. Why not reach out with your hand of faith, receive it, and be made whole?

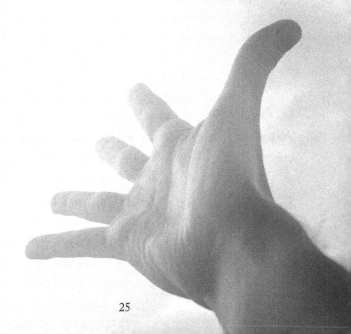

Chapter 2

The Healing Lamb

Old Testament Parables

Paul in the book of First Corinthians 10:6 tells us the stories from the Old Testament are examples to be used in our daily lives and in our sermons. Similar to the use of parables by Jesus, these records of Old Testament stories, heroes, men and women, help to simplify the doctrines of Jesus, Luke, Peter, Paul, James, and John. I often tell ministers that their own stories of deliverance and miracles are fine, but they cannot compare with the use of stories from the Bible to explain the Bible. God not only gives us wonderful doctrines but also examples of those who used them to overcome obstacles we will probably never see. When is the last time you needed an entire sea opened before you because a national army was behind you trying to kill you? When is the last time you were swallowed by a whale? Puts things into perspective, doesn't it?

The First Passover

Who forgives all your iniquities, who heals all your diseases (Psalm 103:3).

There is no more beautiful picture of redemption and healing than the account in Exodus of the first Passover Israel observed before crossing the Red Sea. All Passover meals afterward were observed in the wilderness and Canaan. They were also only remembrances of the first Passover, where God actually delivered Israel from Egypt by killing Egypt's firstborn. God then financially prospered the Israelites and healed every sickness and disease in them before they crossed the Red Sea.

> *He also destroyed all the firstborn in their* [Egypt's] *land, the first of all their strength. He also brought them* [Israel] *out with silver and gold, and there was not one feeble one among His tribes* (Psalm 105:36-37) (Author comments bracketed).

God's Bar Is Set High

Although none of us has arrived to God's standard for our lives, it is still out there. We can strive for it! God's desire is for us to never sin (John 8:11, 2 Peter 1:10, 1 John 2:1), have enough natural prosperity coming into our lives that we can give into every good work (2 Corinthians 9:8), and finally live free from all sickness in continual divine health (3 John 2). Are you there yet? I'm not. But it is still my goal. I have not arrived yet, but I am closer today than I was ten years ago and even five years ago.

Our failures do not cause God to lower His bar, but He encourages each of us to confess our sins, get back up, and get back into the race again. God wants you to set your own bar even with His—no sin, no sickness. He would rather your shoot for the moon and miss it, than to shoot for the ceiling and make it. His Word and His promises have not changed. You would not be told of God's goals for your life if it were not possible for you to reach them. You probably think you have a long way to go, but we all do. The secret is, keep your eyes on how far you have come instead of how far you have to go. Keep increasing, a little at a time, day by day, in righteousness and health.

Four Healing Points

Before we look at the story of Passover from Exodus, let's come back to some foundational points on healing. There are four points I want to present to establish firmly that healing comes from God's grace and not our own works or righteousness.

First, sickness is from Satan and healing comes from God. Jesus "*...went about doing good and healing all who were oppressed by the devil...*" (Acts 10:38).

In other words, sickness is bad, and healing is good. Jesus treated sickness as an enemy. Even the world sees sickness as an enemy. Each day we hear of the battle against breast cancer, heart disease, and Alzheimer's. Why do we fight something if it is our friend? We fight these diseases as our enemies, and one day we expect to look back and find they no longer exist. It takes an ignorant Christian to treat sickness as a friend. God is not the author of sickness. Satan introduced sickness at Adam's fall. Jesus healed "*...all kinds of sickness and all kinds of disease among the people*" (Matthew 4:23) In fact, Jesus healed "*...every sickness and every disease among the people*" (Matthew 9:35).

If some sicknesses comes from God, how did Jesus know who to heal and who to leave alone? On top of that, how did the people know which diseases were all right to bring to Jesus and which were not? They brought every sick person, and Jesus healed every sick person. All sickness and disease came from Satan, and Jesus healed everybody of everything. God's grace is as free to every sick person as it is to every sinful person.

God's grace is as free to every sick person as it is to every sinful person.

Second, creation shows God's attitude toward sickness. Nature serves mankind, all people, good and bad. Plants and animals are our food, and they are also our clothing. But nature also helps to keep us well. Plants and people exchange oxygen for carbon dioxide. What nature breaths out, we breath in and vice versa. Medicines to help cure sickness come from plants and animals. We call aspirin the wonder drug. It has been in willow trees from the Garden of Eden, and we only discovered it a few decades ago. As a gift of God's grace, it was there before we needed it.

Third, our bodies are made in God's image. Grace placed His healing nature in us. Our bodies filter out poisons through our breath, sweat, and waste and keep nutrients from food. God designed our body to keep itself well. Think of all the filtering organs in our body: the lungs, kidneys, liver, appendix, and tonsils. The body, fitfully made, builds up its own immunities to everyday pollution and diseases. Our body rushes to heal itself from destructive attacks. Cut yourself and the body begins healing itself. If harmful bacteria exists in our food, we throw up. Our immune system goes to work and attacks the poisons or disease, then builds up immunities. Our blood contains white cells which attack virus. Coughing, sneezing, and even normal fevers are ways the body expels harmful attacks. So, then, if sickness is God's will, has God taught nature and our body to fight His will? If so, why pay doctors or take medicines to get ourselves out of God's will? No! Healing *is* God's will—*always.*

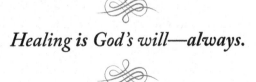

Healing is God's will—always.

Fourth, God's nature is healing. One of God's seven redemptive Old Testament names is healing, *Jehovah Rapha*, "the God who heals us." Nowhere is He called "the God who makes us sick."

When the body cannot heal itself and nature and doctors cannot conquer it, God has healing methods beyond nature. He has given every believer three supernatural gifts for success in healing. First, He sent His Word (healing promises) and healed. Second, He sent His Holy Spirit for our healing: *"The Spirit of the Lord is on me because he has anointed me to heal"* (Luke 4:18). Third, two gifts of the Holy Spirit are for healing—gifts of healings and working of miracles.

Furthermore, Christians can "gang up" on sickness with prayer with the Bible promise: *"If two of you agree on earth concerning anything that they ask, it will be done for them by My Father in heaven"* (Matthew 18:19). *Anything* must include healing for sickness. We can go to prayer meetings to pray for the sick and pray for the sick in the church service, calling for the elders (James 5:14-15).

The Passover Lamb:
The Grace of Healing

He also destroyed all the firstborn in their land [Egypt], the first of all their strength. He also brought them [Israel] out [salvation] with silver and gold [natural blessing], and there was none feeble person among His tribes [heal-ing] (Psalm 105:36-37) (Author comments bracketed).

Something happened between the ten plagues strik-ing Egypt and Israel leaving Egypt sickness free. It was the first Passover.

The Passover Lamb

The lamb has been a symbol of the coming Messiah more than any animal sacrificed by Israel. Jesus was called the "Lamb of God" by John the Baptist (John 1:36) and is seen in heaven as the eternal *"lamb slain from the foundation of the world"* (Revelation 13:8). Jesus Christ is our Passover Lamb (1 Corinthians 5:7), slain for us once and for all.

Just as the shedding of Jesus' blood opened the door for our salvation, healing, and life of victory and blessing here on earth, so it is that the blood of the Passover lamb opened the Red Sea. It was God's leading through the wilderness and eventually the entrance for the Israelites into Canaan. Study of the Passover lamb will help us more than ever to see the grace of God in our healing.

A Perfect Lamb

The lamb chosen for the Passover offering was to be the lamb among lambs. In other words, for three days the chosen lamb was to be examined from front to back and top to bottom. The wool, legs, joints, eyes, ears, heartbeat, and any other parts that could be seen or felt were examined for perfection. Although perfection was not possible, the best was chosen to represent the perfect, virgin-born Lord Jesus Christ, our Passover Lamb to be slain for our sins. The lamb chosen by men for the first Passover meal, represented the future Lamb to come, which would be chosen by God.

The three days of examination by the person offering the lamb represented the three years of public ministry and display Jesus would have before being slain for our sins, healing, and curses on the cross. After examination, God declared His approval twice, saying, *"...This is my beloved Son, in whom I am well pleased"* (Matthew 3:17 and Matthew 17:5). After the first Passover, the lamb was examined by a priest. It is interesting to note that the priest examined the lamb, not the one who brought the lamb. When you come to the Lord in repentance, God examines Jesus—not you. You are declared righteous because of His work—not yours.

The Shedding and Sprinkling of the Blood

On the day the sacrificial lamb was killed, the blood was first put into a bowl and then a small amount was sprinkled on the sides and top of the doorpost leading into the house. The lamb's blood in the bowl represents the blood shed by Jesus for our salvation. The blood sprinkled on the doorpost represents the blood needed in our Christian life for the cleansing of daily sins committed after salvation. A bowl of blood is needed for salvation and only a few drops for cleansing after that. The blood in the bowl protected them from the Lord, the death angel, who went into Egypt to strike the first born (Exodus 12:12-13). The blood over the doorpost protected them from Satan, the destroyer, who would come in while the Lord went into Egypt (Exodus 12:23).

The blood in the bowl represents our salvation, our relationship with God, while the blood over the doorpost represents daily confession of sins, our fellowship with God. Disobedience opened the door for Israel in the wilderness to be attacked by the destroyer (1 Corinthians 10:9-10). Disobedience can do the same in our lives. Repentance, confession of our sins, closes the door to the devil.

Israel Ate All the Lamb before the Exodus

Then they shall eat the flesh on that night; roasted in fire, with unleavened bread and with bitter herbs they shall eat it. Do not eat it raw, nor boiled at all with water, but roasted in fire—its head with its legs and its entrails. You shall let none of it remain until morning, and

what remains of it until morning you shall burn
with fire (Exodus 12:8-10).

Although this does not sound appetizing, only the
blood and waste were removed. *Everything else had to*
be eaten. All the lamb was roasted and eaten. A partial
list would include the skin, organs, kidneys, spleen,
heart, brain, joints, intestines, eyes, and ears. My first
thought would be, *I hope they made it into a stew.*

Why eat it all? *Because the lamb was perfect, and every*
part was perfect. Blind people ate the lamb's eyes, perfect eyes. Deaf people ate the lamb's ears, perfect ears.
Paralyzed people ate the lamb's legs and joints, perfect legs and joints. Mentally ill people ate the lamb's
perfect brain. People with digestive problems ate the
lamb's perfect intestines. When we were born again,
we ate all of Jesus and every one of His perfect parts.
By eating all parts of Him, we have healing for all parts
of us, all our flesh.

> *My son, attend to my words; incline thine ear*
> *unto my sayings. Let them not depart from thine*
> *eyes; keep them in the midst of thine heart. For*

they are life to those that find them and health to **all** *their flesh* (Proverbs 4:20-22 KJV).

And as they were eating, Jesus took bread, blessed and broke it, and gave it to them and said, Take, eat; this is My body" [Eat all of it] (Mark 14:22).

All the Healing You Need Is Already in You

Where do you need healing? That new, perfect part of Jesus is in you. It's not in heaven waiting to be delivered. You have God's righteousness and healing already *in* you. You can choose to walk in the righteousness you already possess, and you can choose to receive the healing already given and present in you.

You have God's righteousness and healing already in you.

> *In Him dwells all the fullness of the Godhead bodily, and you are complete in Him...* (Colossians 2:9-10).

Sounds like healing is as much grace as our salvation.

Chapter 3

The Bible:
Health, Exercise,
and Nutrition

It is somewhat with fear and trembling I enter into this chapter on the biblical perspective of health. The world says, "You are what you eat." This viewpoint not only saturates the secular world but sadly a major portion of the Christian world too. It is only first-world countries that have this attitude. The larger part of the world is not so affluent and blessed to have better sanitary food processing, free-range chickens, and groceries free from genetically modified organisms (GMOs) and pesticides.

Even more sad, we have entire "ministries" based on food, supplements, and warnings of ingredients found in our diets. You dread to eat with them because you will hear a sermon about the ingredients in your choice of food or drink, especially diet colas. I do not believe God intended for us as Christians to spend hours a day examining our food ingredients and how each one is processed and packaged.

Diet and exercise do not produce health. Health comes from God. Simple obedience to His principles produces healing and sustains health. This is true for the whole world, wealthy nations as well as poor. The argument is advanced that it is just common sense that what you eat affects your health. But, when common sense contradicts the Word of God, go with the Word. The Bible view will stand the test of time and common sense will not.

Christian friends of mine, who have written books and spent years recommending certain types of food and supplements, died at younger ages of heart attacks and many times with cancer. Oddly enough, it was cancer they thought they were preventing with their diet and supplements. I really think that fear over food is worse than the food itself. God's plan is simple. Bless with prayer and eat what is put in front of you. Then, spend your days in study of His Word, and tell the world of Jesus' love for them. Or as the prophet Micah put it, *"He has shown you, O man, what is good; And what does the Lord require of you. But to do justly, to love mercy, and to walk humbly with your God"* (Micah 6:8). No mention is made of watching what you eat.

If you disagree or have any prejudgments, read the chapter and compare your thoughts to Scripture. Besides, no one knows you are reading this chapter— just you. All my views on health are from both the Old and New Testament.

There Have Always Been Food Critics

Even in Jesus' day, the Pharisees made lengthy teachings over food, it's preparation, and the washing of hands before eating. Jesus' response made the disciples become concerned over the probable response of the religious leaders.

> So He said to them, "Are you thus without understanding also? Do you not perceive that whatever enters a man from outside cannot defile him, because it does not enter his heart but his stomach, and is eliminated, thus purifying all foods?" And He said, "What comes out of a man, that defiles a man. For from within, out of the heart of men, proceed evil thoughts..." (Mark 7:18-21).

Jesus gives us the whole concept of God's view of eating and spirituality. He had previously told His disciples: "...Out of the abundance of the heart the mouth speaks" (Matthew 12:34).

What comes out of your mouth comes from the heart. In other words, your heart controls your health, not your food. Righteousness and faith-filled words are more important than food. Words of unbelief and fear will defile your health and well-being. You are not what you eat. You are what you think (Proverbs 23:7).

Paul told the same thing to the affluent Romans who were taught by their society the health benefits of eating right. *"The kingdom of God is not eating and drinking, but righteousness and peace and joy in the Holy Spirit"* (Romans 14:17 NASB).

Righteousness is freedom from original sin and a walk of daily holiness. *Peace* is the result of salvation and daily growth in God's Word. *Joy* is a life of praise, worship, and living with the expectation of God's deliverance from all of life's problems. These three do more to keep you in health than examining product labels.

We think we can clean up the food before it goes into our bodies, when Jesus told us in Mark 7:19, *the stomach purifies all foods*. Two problems come from trying to purify our own foods before we eat them. First, our brain is not better at purifying what we eat than our stomach. Our stomach purifies all the food that comes into it and then eliminates the bad ingredients through our waste. Second, if you do not put impurities into your body, how do you build up immunities?

While the food is in your stomach, being purified, the body begins building up immunities. Impurities are needed to have immunities created. If you travel to a foreign country and need an immunization, doctors put a little bit of the disease into your body and within a couple of days, you are immunized. Maybe we have more allergies today because we try to clean up everything with natural foods, filtered water, and cleaner air before we put it into our bodies. A doctor told me that he recommends to every mother to give her children at least one glass of tap water a week. You cannot eliminate impurities from life, but you can build up immunities to them by praying over them and eating what is in front of you. When I was young, if my tootsie roll pop fell out of my mouth, I picked it up and put it back in again. I have been inoculated against earth worms, ants, and dirt. I *think* I'm all right.

Even your body was designed by God's grace. He made your stomach to do the work—not you. Your body is at work whether you think about it and know it or not. You do not have to work to get your digestive system to function, your filtering organs to operate, or your intestines to pass off the waste. Your body will digest food properly even when you sleep. This is grace! But we still work to improve God's plan, trying with our wits to eat healthier.

A Good or Bad Attitude Affects Health—Not Food

Oh, the power and health benefits of joy. *"Then he said to them, 'Go your way, eat the fat* [baby back ribs], *and drink the sweet* [Pepsi], *and send portions to those for whom nothing is prepared; for this day is holy to our Lord. Do not sorrow, for the joy of the Lord is your strength'"* (Nehemiah 8:10) (Author comments bracketed).

Christian fellowship has always been accompanied by good-tasting food and drink. Church picnics are not known for their tofu, filtered water, and vegetable plates. But the joy comes from the fellowship with those attending and the giving of extra food to those who are needy or not present. The joy you have eating and drinking is better for your health than the food.

Or as Solomon put it: *"A merry heart does good, like a medicine, but a broken spirit* [bitterness] *dries the bones"* (Proverbs 17:22) (Author comments bracketed).

Bitterness causes deterioration, the drying of the fountain of your blood, and the bone marrow (Proverbs 3:8). Considering these verses and the health benefits of joy, the one profession which should produce the longest life would be that of a comedian. And it's true. Think of the long lives of George Burns, Bob Hope, and Red Skelton (if you are old enough). Laughter *is* the best medicine.

My mother commented to my sister and I about a story in Reader's Digest many years ago. A man was in the hospital dying of cancer. He asked his daughter to do one thing for him, to bring old movies of the Three Stooges. He hadn't seen them in years and wanted some joy before he died. He could be heard laughing up and down the halls of the hospital, and over the days, his cancer went into remission. Maybe the Bible is right!

Trust and Praise in God's Plan for Your Future Brings Health

Why art thou cast down, O my soul? and why art thou disquieted within me? hope thou in God: for I shall yet praise him, who is the health of my countenance, and my God (Psalm 42:11 KJV).

Confidence in knowing God's future for you will quiet fear and worry, and praise will bring a change of attitude and physical health.

Trust in the Lord with all your heart, and lean not on your own understanding; in all your ways acknowledge Him, and He shall direct your paths. Do not be wise in your own eyes; Fear the Lord and depart from evil. It will be health to you flesh, And strength to your bones (Proverbs 3:5-8).

Knowing you are in God's hands and on His path, lifts responsibility off your shoulders and produces peace. You also experience freedom from arrogance. Walking with God and turning from evil produces and increases health. Health begins in the core of your being (navel) and spreads from there. Walking with God also brings moisture to your bone marrow. These are all symbols of divine health. Solomon has even more to say about trust in God as a source of health. Again, we read from Proverbs 4:20-23:

> *My son, give attention to my words; incline your ear to my sayings. Do not let them depart from your eyes; keep them in the midst of your heart; for they are life to those who find them, and health to all their flesh. Keep your heart with all diligence, for out of it spring the issues of life.*

Notice, out of the heart—not food—flow the issue of life, including health. God's Word contains health for every part of your body. No man-made medicine can cure the entire body. But, by looking at the Word continually, hearing it daily, and hiding it in your heart, health is released to all your flesh. What part of your body is sick? The Word of God, hidden in your heart, will heal it and then give continual health.

Freedom from Strife in the Home Produces Health

An excellent wife is the crown of her husband, but she who causes shame is like rottenness in his bones (Proverbs 12:4).

Solomon says that peace in a marriage can extend the length of your life. Peter also says a good marriage aids your prayer life (1 Peter 3:7).

God's Word contains health for every part of your body.

Telling the Truth Is Healthy

He who speaks truth declares righteousness, but a false witness, deceit. There is one who speaks like the piercings of a sword, but the tongue of the wise promotes health (Proverbs 12:17-18).

The tongue can produce life or death, sickness or health: *"A wholesome tongue is a tree of life, but perverseness in it breaks the spirit"* (Proverbs 15:4).

Encouraging Words from Others Produce Health

A wicked messenger falls into trouble, but a faithful ambassador brings health (Proverbs 13:17).

How a message is presented can produce harm or give health. Giving hope and proper direction, even in a rebuke, can be life changing to someone. Solomon has much more to say on the healing power of a good report.

"The light of the eyes rejoices the heart, and a good report makes the bones healthy" (Proverbs 15:30). A good testimony brings hope to the one who is sick; hope brings healing and health (Psalm 42:11).

The heart of the wise teaches his mouth, and adds learning to his lips. Pleasant words are as an honeycomb, sweetness to the soul, and health to the bones (Proverbs 16:23-24).

Good words bring health to those you speak to, but good words can also bring health to those who speak them. The power of good words from your mouth cannot be taught enough.

Peace Is One of the Greatest Producers of Health

A sound [peaceful, tranquil] *heart is life to the body, but envy is rottenness to the bones* (Proverbs 14:30) (Author comments bracketed).

One of the greatest producers of health is a heart and life at peace. Peace saturates every fiber of your being, bringing health. Anger and jealousy rot the bones, where healthy blood should come from. A clear conscience also produces peace. A clear conscience, and resulting peace, is a great producer of health.

Sharing Your Goods and Home with Others Produces Health

Is it not to share your bread with the hungry, and that you bring to your house the poor who

> *are cast out; when you see the naked, that you*
> *cover him, and not hide yourself from your own*
> *flesh? Then your light shall break forth like the*
> *morning, your healing shall spring forth speed-*
> *ily, and your righteousness shall go before you;*
> *the glory of the Lord shall be your rear guard*
> (Isaiah 58:7-8).

This verse simply tells of the power of love. Sharing your food and clothing with the needy brings health. So does opening your home to the poor.

My mother and father moved to Oklahoma before I was born. They had no place to stay, but a couple who heard of their need, opened their basement to them. They were Christians and my parents were not. They invited my mom and dad to a revival meeting, and they reluctantly accepted out of gratitude for the free room. Both my parents were saved and filled with the Holy Spirit that week, and I consider myself to be in the ministry today because of the generosity of the couple who opened their home to them.

Love in action not only meets the needs of others but also brings health to your own body. Love has wonderful healing powers. Love also has protecting power. Your righteousness will guard you from the front, and the Lord will be your protection from the rear.

Submission and Honor toward Leadership Produces Health

Children, obey your parents in the Lord, for this is right. "Honor your father and mother," which is the first commandment with promise: "that it may be well with you and you may live long on the earth" (Ephesians 6:1-3).

Andrew Wommack said he was watching a National Geographic special on television one night, and they ran a documentary on the longest living group of people found on earth. They were found in the mountains of Japan. The first thing mentioned was their diet. It is so natural to think they must eat something we have not discovered yet. Yet Andrew said the first thing he thought was they honored their parents. In fact, they worship their parents in the religion of Japan. Attitude—not food—produced their health.

Submission toward authority begins with children in the home. This carries them throughout life. They will always have to submit to someone, a boss, policeman, commanding officer, teacher, or pastor. Submission brings with it prosperity and health. The two hands of wisdom include riches and honor, (prosperity) in the left, and length of days (health) in the right (Proverbs 3:16).

Health Comes from the Soul

Beloved, I pray that you may prosper in all things and be in health, just as your soul prospers (3 John 2).

Prosperity of the soul overflows to our financial life and physical health. Again, the heart has more to do with health than diet or exercise.

All Food Comes from God

Now the Spirit expressly says that in latter times some will depart from the faith, giving heed to deceiving spirits and doctrines of demons, speaking lies in hypocrisy, having their own

> *conscience seared with a hot iron, forbidding to*
> *marry, and commanding to abstain from foods*
> *which God created to be received with thanks-*
> *giving by those who believe and know the truth.*
> *For every creature of God is good, and nothing*
> *is to be refused if it is received with thanksgiv-*
> *ing; for it is sanctified by the word of God and*
> *prayer* (1 Timothy 4:1-5).

Paul told Timothy that the closer we come to the return of Jesus, the more we would hear false doctrines and lies from Satan. One of those lies would be the forbidding of certain foods. How many times have we heard warnings against red meat, pork, milk, coffee, eggs, sugar, and fat? After a while we hear they have been found to be all right. Paul called accepting this as *giving heed to seducing spirits.*

The verse says that all foods, meats, and drinks are created by God, and we should receive and eat them with prayer and thanksgiving. God did not plan for prayer over a meal to work until the 21st century. By this time would the additives in food be greater than the power of God in prayer? No. Whatever harm-ful elements are in or on our food are handled by our stomach which purifies all food. If the elements are more harmful than our stomach can purify, prayer over the meal will further sanctify the food. One of God's promises to believers would be, "...*If they drink anything deadly, it will by no means hurt them*" (Mark 16:18).

Health and Fitness

Health comes from God. Health is spiritual not natural. Yet, the health found in the Word of God, and obedience to it, spills over into our natural body. Nowhere in the Bible does it say health comes from diet and exercise. In fact, we have found out it says the exact opposite. Health comes from our heart attitude. So, are diet and exercise addressed anywhere in the Word of God? Of course! I am not saying these are not good, but I am saying they are overrated when compared to God's Word. Fitness is good and does play a part. We will examine Scripture in a moment.

Diet and exercise produce fitness, not health. Fitness is natural rather than spiritual. You can be fit and not healthy. You can also be healthy and not fit. Of course, it is better to be both healthy and fit, but the two are not the same. Many fit people today with very little body fat, who routinely exercise, have had heart attacks and even strokes in young age. Their problem is not a lack of exercise or improper eating but worry and stress. On the other hand, many people who are not fit are nonetheless healthy. All their vital signs seem to be in acceptable ranges. I heard that doctors are calling this group of people obese-healthy. Being moderately over-weight is not necessarily an indicator of poor health.

Health comes from God.
Health is spiritual not natural.

What about Food and the Bible?

The only sin attached to eating in the Bible is not *what* you eat, but *how much* you eat. With both the eating of food and the drinking of wine, excess is a sin, not indulging. *"Be not drunk with wine, wherein is excess..."* (Ephesians 5:18 KJV).

One of the fruits of the Holy Spirit is *temperance*, not prohibition. Anything in life that is good can become bad. Excessiveness can turn the good thing into a sin. All food is given by God to be eaten, not over indulged in. Eating and drinking smaller amounts will bring your weight into balance and keep it there. This is good natural thinking and spiritual thinking as well.

What about Exercise and the Bible?

Since fitness is temporary, it must be constantly reinforced. Diets must be continually monitored, and exercise must become a way of life.

> *For bodily exercise profits a little* [briefly, for a short while], *but godliness is profitable for all things, having promise of the life that now is and of that which is to come* (1 Timothy 4:8).

If you begin an exercise program, you must stick with it. When you stop, you lose all the ground you gained. But on the other hand, First Timothy tells us, one revelation from God's Word can change your life forever. It can affect your earthly life until you die and then you can carry that revelation into eternity.

All this verse is saying is, don't go overboard on the natural (diet and exercise), but do go overboard on the spiritual. Both the natural and spiritual have their place, but get your priorities straight. The first is natural and temporary. The second is spiritual and eternal. Health comes from God, not your stomach or your workouts at the gym. It is by grace.

> *For by grace you have been saved* [sozo][healed] *through faith, and that not of yourselves; it is the gift of God, not of works...* (Ephesians 2:8-9) (Author comments bracketed).

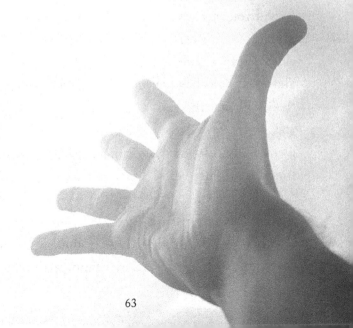

Chapter 4

You Cannot Add to God's Perfect Plan

God's Plan Sounds Too Good to Be True

Truly, this only have I found: That God made man upright, but they have sought out many schemes [their own devices] (Ecclesiastes 7:29) (Author comments bracketed).

Solomon came to the same conclusion we all as Christians have come to: We think God's plans often seem too good to be true, and we believe we have to add our own ideas to improve His.

Did you ever wonder why God made man last when He restored the earth and the Garden of Eden? All the atmosphere, clouds, animals, fish, birds, trees, plants, and food were already made when God placed Adam in the Garden at the end of the sixth day. Why did God wait so long? So man couldn't help. So it is with each plan of God for us. He planned for every answer we would need long before we were born or our problems existed. This was even before the foundation and creation of the universe and earth. We cannot have a need God has not already seen ahead of time and created an answer to meet. Our salvation, healing, natural needs of food, finances, and problems of life are already seen as met. We can walk into a problem knowing the way of escape was already there. The way of escape was there before the problem existed.

God has never been taken by surprise when something went wrong. God does not make up answers when a need arises. He plans for the answer when He knows a problem will come. He is omniscient, and therefore, knows all things good and bad that will come. He was not surprised when Lucifer rose up to try and overthrow Him. He already had a plan to turn around Lucifer's rebellion. He was not surprised when Adam and Eve ate the fruit and threw the whole world into sin and death. He had a plan for another Adam to come along, Jesus Christ, and undo what the first Adam had done. So it is in our own life. God does not create our problems. Satan, our flesh, other people and the world are responsible for them. But God does create every answer to every problem.

But We Still Try to Improve God's Plan

We believe salvation comes by faith in Jesus Christ, but we try to improve the plan by adding: "be water baptized," "join our church," or "tithe to our church." All these are fine and even commanded in the Word of God, but they are not commanded in order for us to be saved. What would the poor thief crucified next to Jesus have done if he had to do any of these things? He was crucified with nails and a few minutes away from death. He could not have got off the cross, found a church, walked down the aisle, been water baptized, or given an offering. Yet Jesus still told him he would be in paradise by the end of that day.

Who was the first one who tried to add to God's perfect plan with his own scheme? It was Adam. God told him that he and Eve were not to eat the fruit of the tree. But by the time Satan tempted the woman, she added *"...nor shall we touch it..."* (Genesis 3:3). Where did she hear this from? She was not yet made when God gave the command to Adam. Adam must have added it to keep her further away from the tree and the fruit. When she touched it, nothing happened, so she ate. Our additions to God's commands confuse the issue and make matters worse.

Forgiveness and Grace

I have heard it taught that God will not forgive you unless you promise not to commit the sin again. Jesus does not forgive a sin only once and never again. He even said we are to forgive others more than seven times, even until seventy times seven (Matthew 18:21-22). We do not quit committing a certain sin by promising never to do it again. We quit sinning by growing up. This may involve confessing the same sin a number of times. God is always faithful and just to forgive us (1 John 1:9).

We quit sinning by growing up.

Healing and Grace

I also heard a minister who was used mightily in divine healing tell people in a prayer line that he would not pray for them if they were overweight. He said, "God will not heal you of things that are your own fault." He told them to come back after they had lost weight and he would pray for them. In fact, he said if they lost weight, they would probably never have the problem again and would not need prayer.

This is so unscriptural it hurts to think about it. All sins are our fault. No sin sneaks up on us and forces us to rebel against God. Food does not jump in our mouth and make us overeat. We allow it to happen. Yet Jesus will forgive us and heal us. Jesus healed everyone who came to Him of every sickness and disease (Matthew 4:23-24, 9:35). You would think one or more of them were overweight. I'm sure tobacco and illegal drugs existed in Jesus' day and many came with resulting health problems. Jesus did not tell any of them to stop overeating or to drop their death-producing habits. He healed them by His grace and mercy, motivated by compassion (Matthew 14:14).

After Jesus prayed for them, He often told them to "sin no more," but if they did, I am sure He would pray for them again. Think of the people who brought in the multitudes for healing. They did not find some people who were overweight or obviously abusing their bodies and tell them they could not come for healing. They did not find those who had been healed before and sinned again and tell them they could not be prayed for again.

There is no disease God will not heal, including the ones that are our fault. There is no sin God will not save us from and forgive us of, even the ones that are our fault. The "all" who came to Him for healing are no different than the "all" who are alive today.

The promise still stands today: *"Who forgives all your iniquities, Who heals all your diseases"* (Psalm 103:3).

Why will we tell a sinner that Jesus has already judged their sins on the cross and will forgive them all if they will just receive Him as their Savior? While, at the same time, we judge and examine sick people to see if they are "worthy" of our prayers for their healing. When I pray for people in a healing service, and they seem to act unworthy, I tell them to simply open up and receive healing as grace, not because they deserve or merit it. We do not deserve the forgiving of our sins or the healing of our bodies. *"For by grace you have been saved* [sozo—healed and delivered also] *through faith, and that not of yourselves; it is the gift of God"* (Ephesians

2:8) (Author comments bracketed). So, how can you prepare yourself for healing? You cannot! Come as you are! Or as we sing it "just as I am."

But at Times, Forgiveness and Healing Are United

I know some of you are thinking, like I would, *The scriptures say that sin will stop the healing power of God from coming into our lives.* This is true, but it is not the sin necessarily that stops the healing but rather our unrepentant attitude toward the sin, those who sinned against us, or even toward ourselves. Jesus cleared up this topic on a number of occasions. Let's look at one.

> *Then behold, they brought to Him a paralytic lying on a bed. When Jesus saw their faith, He said to the paralytic, "Son, be of good cheer; your sins are forgiven you." And at once some of the scribes said within themselves, "This Man blasphemes!" But Jesus, knowing their thoughts, said, "Why do you think evil in your hearts? For which is easier, to say, 'Your sins are forgiven you,' or to say, 'Arise and walk'? But that you*

> *may know that the Son of Man has power on earth to forgive sins"—then He said to the paralytic, "Arise, take up your bed, and go to your house." And he arose and departed to his house* (Matthew 9:2-7).

The reason why grace applies to healing as well as forgiveness of sins is because Jesus told us healing is an outward manifestation of inward forgiveness (vs 6). Healing is physical proof Jesus can forgive sins. It is no more difficult for Jesus to heal disease than to forgive sin. Both are impossible for men. Both are possible for God. What Jesus saw from the men who brought this paralytic to Him was their faith. What was missing was grace. Something stood in the way of this man receiving healing; it was his lack of understanding of God's grace.

This is why Jesus told the man in verse 2, *"Take heart, my son. Your sins are forgiven"* (ESV). The key to what Jesus said is found in the Greek. The word forgiven, *aphiemi*, is in the perfect tense. It comes across in the English as past tense, but that is only half of the meaning. The other half is present tense. The perfect tense is a mixture of the past and present tense. The action happened in the past, but the results keep coming up to this present minute. It is the same as Ephesians 2:8, *"For by grace are you saved* [perfect tense]..." (Author comments bracketed). It refers to a person being saved in the past with results that keep coming up to the present. You don't have to get saved again. Rejoice that when you were saved, you have been in a constant state of salvation ever since.

What Jesus told the man was, "Son, your sins have been forgiven from the time you asked." The problem with the man was not that God had not forgiven his sins but that he could not forgive himself. His guilt had kept him from receiving his healing. Jesus' words must have swept through his mind like a cleansing wave. He suddenly saw God's grace and his healing was immediate. Not all sickness is a result of personal sins, but all sickness is a result of original sin, the fall of Adam, and the curse released in the earth. God not only wants to save us from our sins but also from sinning. He saves us from sin, but we must accept the gift of His Son, Jesus. He saves us from daily sins (sinning) by confessing (admitting) our sins, growing up in His Word, and walking daily in the Spirit.

Your word I have hidden in my heart, that I might not sin against You (Psalm 119:11).

...Walk in the Spirit, and you shall not fulfill the lust of the flesh (Galatians 5:16).

Does God Forgive and Heal Us to Sin and Abuse Ourselves Again?

Of course, the answers to both these questions is "no." God forgives and heals us because He loves us. He then wants us to be filled with so much gratitude that we begin a new walk toward righteousness and health. "*...Shall we sin continue in sin, that grace may abound? God forbid* [emphatically not]..." (Romans 6:1-2 KJV) (Author comments bracketed). Because we are no longer under the law does not mean we are free to live by our flesh. If I love my wife, I do not commit adultery. Because I love the Lord, I do not sin against Him. "*...Shall we sin because we are not under the law but under grace?* (Romans 6:15). Emphatically not!

After Forgiveness, Grace Is Accompanied with a Warning

In John 8:1-11, the woman caught in adultery was brought to Jesus to see if He would remain true to the law and have her stoned to death. Jesus operated in grace toward her and brought up the law to the men. He forgave her so He could also forgive the men. If she was to be stoned, then so should they. When Jesus reminded them of their own sins, they walked away one by one, leaving only Jesus and the woman. After forgiving her, He said, *"...Neither do I condemn you; go and sin no more"* (vs. 11). Jesus did not say she had not sinned, but He let her know her sins were forgivable. Faced with unmerited grace, Jesus commanded her to leave and not sin again. God does not forgive us to sin again but to be strengthened to not sin again.

God's grace teaches *"...us that, denying ungodliness and worldly lusts, we should live soberly, righteously, and godly in this present age"* (Titus 2:12). Forgiveness and healing should wake us up to a life of godly living, not more sinning. This woman, caught in the very act of adultery, was forgiven and told not to sin again.

Forgiveness is an open door to healing, and sin is an open door for more sickness and evil consequences.

After Healing, Grace Is Accompanied with a Warning

In John 5:2-14, we have the story of the paralytic waiting for the moving of the water. He waited to be lowered in the pool, so he could be healed by an angel from heaven. Jesus spoke to him and told him to, "*...Rise, take up your bed and walk*" (vs 8). He did rise up and walk and later saw Jesus again who told him, "*...Sin no more, lest a worse thing come upon you*" (vs 14). Jesus did not condemn him, but He also did not fail to warn him of the consequences of continued sin. God's mercy heals like it forgives—not by works. Forgiveness is an open door to healing, and sin is an open door for more sickness and evil consequences. If this man would have sinned again, and a sickness or worse disease come on him, would Jesus have healed him again? The answer is yes, and Jesus would have warned him again not to sin.

In heaven I will meet the woman caught in adultery and the paralyzed man who both had the Lord tell them not to sin again. I trust I will find out they both took heed and began a life toward holiness out of appreciation for what God had done for them through the forgiving and healing ministry of Jesus. The grace of God was shown to them to forgive and heal each one and teach them not to sin.

Under Jesus ministry, those who had willfully sinned were forgiven, including liars, thieves, fornicators, and homosexuals. Also, those whose sicknesses were self-inflicted were healed, including wrong eaters, overeaters, smokers, alcoholics, and drug abusers. Have you been forgiven for things that were your fault?

The answer should be yes! Have you been healed for sicknesses that were self-inflicted? Again, the answer should be yes! Have you sinned again? Of course, you have. But I trust you are living stronger for Jesus today than you were at the time. Has Jesus been faithful and just to forgive you of sins since then? The answer is, again, yes! Then, *"If you love Me, keep My command-ments"* (John 14:15).

Epaphraditus Was Sick by His Own Actions

Since he was longing for you all, and was distressed because you had heard that he was sick. For indeed he was sick almost unto death; but God had mercy on him, and not only on him but on me also, lest I should have sorrow on sorrow. Because for the work of Christ he came close to death, not regarding his life, to supply what was lacking in your service toward me (Philippians 2:26-27,30).

Epaphroditus was sick because he would not take off time from his work of ministering to people. He worked his body into a state of exhaustion and was close to death. God raised him back up by His mercy. In other words, God healed him because of grace not because he deserved to be healed. He abused his own body and he and Paul admitted it to the people. God gave him a new start and a second chance to finish his ministry.

Both healing and forgiveness are a fresh start on a new life, not a chance to go back to your ways of sin. God's desire is that you not sin again. But He also has made provision for forgiveness and healing if you confess the sins and accept the grace of forgiveness and healing.

Make up your mind to use your healing to turn from sin and not take the opportunity to sin again. Use your healing to be a blessing and minister to others. When Peter's mother in law was healed, Jesus touched her hand, and "...*she rose up and served them*" (Matthew 8:14-15). Use your forgiveness and healing to be gracious to others as you have received grace yourself.

Chapter 5

Everyone of Everything

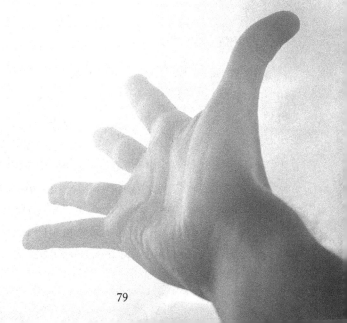

All Diseases in All the People

*Jesus went about all Galilee, teaching in their synagogues, preaching the gospel of the kingdom, and **healing all kinds of sickness** and **all kinds of disease** among the people. Then His fame went throughout all Syria; and they brought to Him **all sick people** who were afflicted with various diseases and torments, and those who were demon-possessed, epileptics, and paralytics; and **He healed them. Great** multitudes followed Him—from Galilee, and from Decapolis, Jerusalem, Judaea, and beyond the Jordan* (Matthew 4:23-25).

This verse is the first of two bookends of Jesus' healing ministry in Matthew, the other comes in Matthew 9:35. Between the two bookends Jesus healed every type of person of every type of sickness. Jesus began His healing ministry in His home area of Galilee in the Jewish synagogues. He spoke in large cities and small villages. Yet, His message was the same in each. He preached to sinners, taught to believers, and healed every person of every sickness. His fame began to expand to Greek cities and beyond the Jordan to Gentile countries. The Greek word for fame is *akoe*, where we get our word *acoustics*. The message of Jesus' healing ministry was spread by word of mouth, day after day. His fame spread from one city and village to another, until the crowds were so huge, Jesus had to take time off, go to a mountain apart, and teach His disciples how to handle this expanding ministry. When Jesus came down from the mountain, the multitudes had grown even more and Jesus continued healing every sickness and every disease among everyone who came to Him (Matthew 9:35).

To Everyone Who Believes

Healing everyone of every disease shows God's grace attached to our need of healing. Like grace forgives every person of every sin who comes to Him, so it is with anything which comes through Jesus' cross. This includes forgiveness of sins, the natural provisions of life, and physical healing. *"Who forgives all your iniquities, who heals all your diseases"* (Psalm 103:3).

> *For I am not ashamed of the gospel of Christ, for*
> *it is the power of God to salvation for everyone*

who believes, for the Jew first and also for the Greek (Romans 1:16).

The removal of our sins and the giving of eternal life come through the gospel and are received by faith. So it is with healing. Part of the gospel to be taken into all the world includes divine healing: *"...They will lay hands on the sick, and they shall recover"* (Mark 16:18).

Kenneth E. Hagin said, "Healing is the dinner bell for the gospel." People who receive their healing by faith are now ready to receive the Giver of healing by faith, Jesus as their Savior. Since salvation is by grace, so is healing. The beauty is, like forgiveness of sins, our healing is already complete, seen by God as already done. We also need to see it done and just receive it.

Individual Cases of Healing

In Matthew 4, Jesus healed multitudes of people of every disease. In the next three chapters, He trained His disciples at the sermon on the mount (chapters 5-7) to handle the crowds needing ministering and healing. In the next two chapters (8-9), we have individual cases of healing to amplify the fact that Jesus heals everyone of everything. When Jesus healed the multitudes, He could not have laid hands on them because of the huge numbers who needed healing. Jesus must have only spoken the Word, told the people to receive their healing, and saw everyone healed of every disease.

In Matthew chapters 8 and 9, Jesus takes on individual cases and lays His hands on most of them. Let's look at each case.

A Leper (Matthew 8:1-4)

Jesus' first personal case of healing was a leper. A leper is a type of sinner, and leprosy is a type of sin. The disease was incurable in its day. In fact, healing a leper was not called healing but *cleansing.* The curing of a leper seems to be more attached to the work of Jesus' blood and not the stripes on His body. Jesus separated the leper from all other forms of sickness when He told His disciples, *"Heal the sick, cleanse the leper..."* (Matthew 10:8). Although the leper truly was healed of his leprosy, it was called a *cleansing.* The first thing the leper asked Jesus was if He was *willing* to cleanse him of the leprosy. He knew Jesus *could* cleanse him. Jesus told him without hesitation, "I will." Jesus touched the man and immediately the leprosy was cleansed. Jesus then told him to show himself to the priest, as a testimony to them, before he showed himself healed to other people. This was commanded by Moses in Leviticus 14.

The Centurion's Servant (Matthew 8:5-13)

A Roman centurion was the second one who came to ask healing for his paralyzed servant. It is also recorded of this officer that he had received the Lord of Israel and, with his personal wealth, had built a synagogue for the Jewish people. These acts did not save him but were an outward proof of his personal trust in Christ. In fact, Jesus commended the man for his faith and even declared He had not found this amount of faith in the Jews of Israel.

Peter's Mother-in-law (Matthew 8:14-15)

Peter's mother-in-law had a fever. This healing was not as dramatic as deliverance from leprosy or paralysis but was nonetheless impossible for anyone to heal. We often see disease as small and large, but God sees them all the same. Small sins and big sins are both only cleansed by the blood of Jesus and not by us. Just as we cannot forgive our own sins, we also cannot heal our own diseases, even the smallest ones. Jesus touched the woman's hand and rebuked her fever. She was healed and rose up to minister to those who were with Jesus. Healing always should be used to minister to others.

The fact that Jesus took her by the hand is striking. In almost every case, Jesus touched women on the hand and not on any other part of the body. Jesus was very discreet in how he ministered to women, even with a dead, young girl He raised to life.

The Woman with the Issue of Blood (Matthew 9:20-22)

This woman had been sick with a female problem for twelve years. She had gone to many doctors and spent all that she had looking for a cure and had found none. This woman was not touched by Jesus but touched Him herself. The healing virtue (*dunamis*, power) that surround Jesus flowed into her, and she was healed of the disease immediately. Jesus had her remain long enough to give her testimony. Jesus told her that her faith had made her *whole*. The Greek word for *whole* means that any other effects of the disease were also removed. She was completely whole.

It is interesting to note that Jesus did not chastise her for going to doctors. God is not against doctors, and Jesus did not refuse to heal her because she had already been to a doctor. Doctors are not against God's will but are fully accepted by Him. Paul traveled with Luke, an apostle traveling with a medical doctor. Two books of the New Testament were written by Doctor Luke. If doctors are a sin, then God called Himself a sinful name. Because the Lord Himself is called a doctor in the Old Testament, the Lord who heals *(Rapha)*, the "Great Physician" (Exodus 15:26).

Jairus' Daughter (Matthew 9:23-25)

Jairus had approached Jesus to come to his house and heal his daughter before Jesus was touched by the woman with the issue of blood. Because Jesus took time to listen to her testimony, Jairus' daughter died before the testimony was finished. Jairus was tempted to ask Jesus not to come to heal her at that point because she was dead, but Jesus told him that all things were possible. All Jairus had to do was believe and death could be conquered like any sickness or disease. Jesus went to the house, ran the mourners out of the room, touched the dead girl's hand, and she came back to life. Jesus not only gives healing but also resurrection to the lifeless.

Two Blind Men (Matthew 9:27-30)

Jesus went into the house of the blind men and asked them if they believed Jesus could heal them. They responded "yes" and were healed and could see based on their simple confession of faith in Jesus' power to heal. I love this part of the story. Jesus told them not to tell anyone, and they immediately went out and told as many as possible. Times have not changed.

A Mute (Matthew 9:32-33)

This man who could not speak was controlled by a demon which kept him from speaking. Jesus cast out the demon, and the man could speak immediately. This was done before a great crowd of onlookers and Pharisees, and they all marveled at what Jesus had done. The Pharisees claimed Jesus was casting out demons by Satan's power.

Seven Cases, All Different

These healing cases amplify the verses that tell us Jesus healed all people of all diseases (Matthew 4:23, 9:35).

There is not a single case where we cannot identify. The first case, a leper, was an older man, Jewish, incurable, and poor. The second case was a young man, a Roman and a Gentile, paralyzed and wealthy. He was healed from a distance by the faith of someone else. The third case was a woman, a Jew, a housewife, who had a fever for only a short time. The fourth case was a younger woman, with a female problem, twelve years sick, who had visited doctors but was healed when she touched Jesus' clothes. The fifth case was a young girl who had already died but Jesus raised to life again. The sixth case actually included two blind men who Jesus healed at the same time. The seventh case was a mute and demon-possessed man.

Let's review. Jesus healed old men, young boys, old women, young girls, Jews, Gentiles, incurable lepers, paralytic cases to fevers, poor, rich, living, dead, military men, housewives, those who had been to doctors and those who had not, the sick, the demon-possessed, one at a time, more than one at a time, and multitudes at a time. What's your excuse?

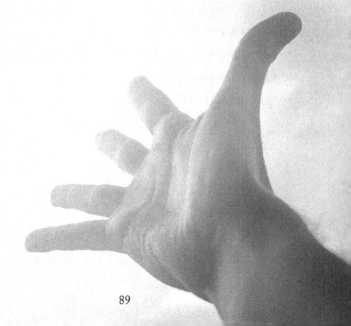

Chapter 6

That It Might
Be Fulfilled

Isaiah Foretold of Jesus Bearing Our Sicknesses

When evening had come, they brought to Him many who were demon-possessed. And He cast out the spirits with a word, and healed all who were sick, that it might be fulfilled which was spoken by Isaiah the prophet [Isaiah 53:4], *saying: "He Himself took our infirmities and bore our sicknesses"* (Matthew 8:16-17) (Author comments bracketed).

In the midst of individual healings in Matthew chapters 8 and 9, this verse is quoted from Isaiah as the basis for Jesus being able to heal all who came to Him of every disease. This passage in Matthew 8 has been very controversial among scholars who do not believe Jesus took our sickness on the cross along with our sins. They believe Jesus only took our sins when He died for us. They teach that our pains and sicknesses *can* be healed, but it is outside the work of the cross. In other words, healing is left to the sovereignty of God, not the grace of God. The Holy Spirit, through Matthew, correctly translates the two Hebrew words in Isaiah

53:4, *koilia* and *makob* as "infirmities" and "sicknesses," instead of "griefs" and "sorrows." In Isaiah 53, verse 4 addresses our sicknesses and verse 5 addresses our sins.

The cross cries out loudly of the grace of God. And anything which comes by way of the cross arrives to us through God's grace and is available simply through our faith. Many scholars say anyone can trust God for salvation, but one has to wait on God's sovereign will to be displayed for healing. It is also taught by these teachers that if you are not saved, it is not God's fault but yours. You simply did not receive what was available for all mankind. But if you do not receive healing after asking for it, it is not your fault but God's choice. His sovereign will for you was not to be healed. Again, if you remove any work of Jesus from the cross, you remove it from God's plan of grace.

But Healing Is Also a Grace

But the Holy Spirit emphatically included healing as part of Jesus' work for us on the cross. He took a verse that scholars only attribute to salvation and said it included healing of all our diseases as well as salvation from all our sins. Jesus said on many occasions that the healing was manifested in the bodies of those who were sick because of their faith. He told the woman with the issue of blood, *"...Daughter, your faith has made you well. Go in peace, and be healed of your affliction"* (Mark 5:34). The lame man at the Gate Beautiful was raised up and made whole by his faith in Jesus' name (Acts 3:16). Jesus told the leader of the synagogue, concerning the raising up of his daughter from the dead, *"...Do not be afraid; only believe"* (Mark 5:36). Faith receives what God gives in grace.

In Grace, Jesus Took Our Place so We Could Take His Place

A story is told in Genesis 48 of the events just before the death of Jacob. He called Joseph to bring his sons before him so he could bless them. In the next chapter, he called his sons to surround him so he could bless them and their children also. He prophesied over each of the sons, telling them of blessing and cursing which would face them and their tribes in the centuries to come before the Messiah, Shiloh, would come to rule the earth. But the first grandsons Jacob blessed were the two sons of Joseph who were born to him and his Egyptian wife in Egypt.

In Genesis 48:8-14, Joseph placed the older grandson in his left arm so he would be in front of Jacob's right hand to receive the blessings of the firstborn. Of course, then, the younger son was in his right arm to be in front of Jacob's left hand. While Joseph had his eyes closed, Jacob crossed his hands and put his right hand on the younger, recalling the words over him in his mother's womb, "...*the older shall serve the younger*" (Genesis 25:23). When Joseph opened his eyes and saw what his father was doing, he tried to remove and rearrange his hands. Jacob simply told Joseph that he knew what he was doing.

God Crossed His Hands for Our Righteousness

On the cross, Jesus, the elder son, voluntarily took the curse we possessed so we could voluntarily accept the righteousness He possessed. God crossed hands and put our sins on His eldest Son and placed His righteousness on us. Jesus chose to accept, and we are to do the same.

God crossed His hands over Jesus and us, for the removal of our sins and for the giving of Jesus' righteousness.

> *He* [the Father] *made Him* [Jesus] *who knew no sin to be sin for us, that we might be made the righteousness of God in Him* (2 Corinthians 5:21) (Author comments bracketed).

The older son of Joseph did not deserve the lesser blessing, and the younger did not deserve the blessings of the firstborn. But Jacob knew what he was doing. Jesus did not deserve the curses of Adam being given to Him, and we did not deserve the blessings of Jesus being given to us. But God the Father knew what He was doing. Jesus took the sins of everyone so everyone could receive His righteousness. *"Who forgives all your iniquities..."* (Psalm 103:3).

God Crossed His Hands for Our Healing

The opening verse in this chapter from Matthew 8 tells us Jesus bore our sicknesses and took our infirmities. This is on the same cross Jesus took our sins and iniquities. If all we must do to be saved is receive Jesus' gift of righteousness, then all we have do to be healed is receive Jesus' gift of healing. God crossed hands and gave Jesus our sicknesses and pains with one, and with the other, gave Jesus' healing to us. God's grace on the cross is released to us through simple faith in His promise of salvation and healing. "...*Who heals all your diseases*" (Psalm 103:3).

> *Jesus did not forget a sin or overlook a disease. He conquered every one of them on the cross.*

Grace Will Never Have to Be Repeated

What I mean is that what Jesus did on the cross was finished and will never have to be done again. Jesus did not forget a sin or overlook a disease. He conquered every one of them on the cross. Now, Jesus *"...dies no more..."* (Romans 6:9) and neither do we.

What Jesus did for us on the cross was seen in the heart of God as already done before the foundation of the world, before the cross was an historical fact. This is why people could be saved and healed in the Old Testament before Jesus actually came and completed the work on the cross. Abraham was saved by faith because he *"believed in the Lord, and He* [God] *accounted it to him for righteousness"* (Romans 4:22, see Genesis 15:6) (Author comments bracketed). David was saved the same way and said, *"Blessed are those whose lawless deeds are forgiven, and whose sins are covered; blessed is the man to whom the Lord shall not impute sin"* (Romans 4:6-8).

Isaiah 9:6, prophesying of the work of Jesus on the cross said, *"For unto us a Child is born, unto us a Son is given."* The *us's* of this verse were five hundred years before the Child was born or the Son given. Yet, salvation and healing were available to them based on what Jesus was yet to do.

So it is with Jesus' healing ministry. Matthew 8:16-17 says, *"Himself took our infirmities and bore our sicknesses."*

Jesus had not yet gone to the cross but counted healing as an already finished work. Both *took* and *bore* are past tense. The Man to whom the verses was referring stood in front of the people to heal them and had not even gone to the cross yet to bring it to pass. Yet, God saw it as already accomplished. Grace was provided before the world began and is such an accomplished fact that God healed the people on the work Jesus was yet to do. Jesus was seen as the Lamb slain before the foundation of the world. Anything connected to the cross has already been done, and our works cannot improve or add to it to make it come to pass. On the cross, Jesus said, *"It is finished."* He accomplished that day what God had counted as already done. When you receive forgiveness of sins or healing of any disease, you fulfill in your life what God accomplished before the world began.

Receive Remission of Sins and Receive Your Healing

If healing is already done, you do not have to ask God for it. Grace is not asked for, expecting God to then do something. Grace is received, knowing God has already accomplished and provided it. You do not have to ask God to save you. Receive your salvation! You do not have to ask God to heal you. Receive your healing! The hand of grace, filled with forgiveness and healing, is held out to you. With your empty hand of faith, reach out and receive what God provided for you through the cross of Jesus, forgiveness of every sin and healing of every disease.

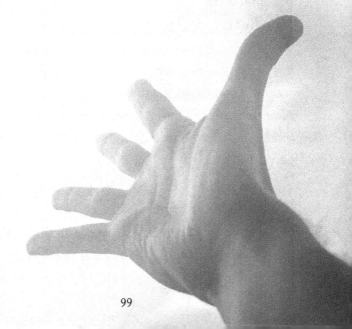

Chapter 7

The Year of Jubilee

The Holy Spirit and Healing

When Jesus introduced His public ministry to His hometown of Nazareth, He spoke of the power of the Holy Spirit given to Him to forgive sins and heal sickness. I have spent much time teaching of the Scriptures being fulfilled concerning our healing, but the other half of the healing equation is the Holy Spirit. The Word of God and the Holy Spirit agree and work together to accomplish the will of God in our lives.

In salvation, we believe the Word of God, the gospel, for it is the "...*power of God to salvation...*" (Romans 1:16). But then it is the Holy Spirit who takes our faith in the gospel, quickens us, and gives us eternal life. So it is with healing. When we receive God's Word, His scriptures on divine healing, we believe what God has promised to us. The Holy Spirit then gives life to the diseased part of our body and delivers God's healing power to us.

Grace is God's part to deliver to us forgiveness of sins and healing of our diseases. There are no works on our part, but there is a responsibility. We must receive God's grace by faith. Jesus' work on the cross was for the entire world, but faith makes that work personal—just for us. Again, grace is God reaching out to us with all things that pertain to our natural life and spiritual life. Faith is our part to reach out and receive God's grace.

The Acceptable Year of the Lord

So He came to Nazareth, where He had been brought up. And as His custom was, He went into the synagogue on the Sabbath day, and stood up to read. And He was handed the book of the prophet Isaiah. And when He had opened the book, He found the place where it was written: "The Spirit of the Lord is upon Me, because He has anointed Me to preach the gospel to the poor; He has sent Me to heal the brokenhearted, to proclaim liberty to the captives and recovery of sight to the blind, to set at liberty those who are oppressed; to proclaim the acceptable year of the Lord." Then He closed the book, and gave it back to the attendant and sat down. And the eyes of all who were in the synagogue were fixed on Him. And He began to say to them,

"Today this Scripture is fulfilled in your hearing." So all bore witness to Him, and marveled at the gracious words which proceeded out of His mouth. And they said, "Is this not Joseph's son?" (Luke 4:16-22).

Jesus had spent thirty years in private, in study of the Word, and in preparation for three years of public ministry. The door into this public ministry came when the Holy Spirit descended on Him as He was being baptized by John (John 1:32-34). With the Word of God and the power of the Holy Spirit, Jesus was then prepared to accomplish God's will through His life: forgiveness of sins and healing of sickness.

Jesus proclaimed from Isaiah 61:1-2 six things He was, from that point on, prepared to do through the ministry of the Holy Spirit.

1. He was sent to preach the gospel to the poor, which includes those with both spiritual and natural bankruptcy. Jesus mentioned the "poor in spirit" in Matthew 5:11 as those who needed to be redeemed from the bankruptcy of sin

and Adam's transgression. Paul taught us in Second Corinthians 8:9 that Jesus became poor for us that we might be made rich. The "we" he spoke to had already been saved and redeemed from spiritual poverty. This means Jesus also died so we could be rich in the natural abundance of life, not so we could heap it on ourselves but use our riches to give into the gospel and supply for the needs of others. The Word instructs us that, *"God is able to make all grace abound toward you, that you, always having all sufficiency in all things, may have an abundance for every good work"* (2 Corinthians 9:8).

2. Jesus was sent to heal the brokenhearted. We often think of healing as just physical, but emotional healing is also found in the work of Jesus. Think of the emotional relief that came to the man who was paralyzed when Jesus told him his sins were forgiven and to rise and walk. When the woman caught in adultery was

alone with Jesus, He told her He did not condemn her but to go and sin no more. How wonderful and relieved she must have felt. Depression, confusion, bitterness, and anger are only a few of the healings Jesus wants to deliver us from. If fact, many of our physical diseases are a result of emotional turmoil. To free a broken heart is often to help a person find physical health.

3. Jesus was sent to preach deliverance to the captives. This not only speaks of natural slavery but also of spiritual slavery to Satan and demons. Jesus healed a daughter of Abraham who had been bound by Satan for eighteen years. Every demon-possessed unbeliever and demon-controlled believer Jesus freed were delivered from their spiritual captivity.

4. Jesus was sent for recovery of sight to the blind. This is physical healing of which Jesus accomplished on the multitudes and

individuals He met in His ministry. He healed *all* who came to Him.

5. Jesus was sent to set at liberty those who were bruised. This includes those who have emotional scars from the wickedness of Satan and those in the world. This is from abusive fathers, mothers, husbands, wives, and others who said and allowed unthinkable things to be done. Jesus not only can forgive of those things but also heal from the memories of them. No one went through more rejection and abuse than Jesus Himself. Jesus is touched with the feelings of our infirmities. And He cannot only identify, but He can heal.

6. Jesus was sent to preach the acceptable year of the Lord. This is a reference to the Year of Jubilee.

The Year of Jubilee

After Jesus mentioned Jubilee, He closed the book of Isaiah and told the crowd, this scripture was fulfilled that day in their ears. The people eventually became angry at Jesus but not before they had one other reaction. They "...*marveled at the gracious words which proceeded out of His mouth...*" (Luke 4:22). Before applying natural thinking to Jesus' statements, they were struck by God's grace through His words. Every one of the blessings Jesus spoke of required nothing on their part. Each one was a gift from God for the taking. This included the "...*acceptable year of the Lord,*" (Luke 4:19) the Year of Jubilee.

I'm sure the anger that arose in the people against Jesus probably began with the thought, *This can't be right. Jubilee is many years away.* Then they began thinking of Jesus as the carpenter's son their children grew up with, the very one they had known for years. Familiarity breeds contempt, and contempt was abundant at that moment.

But what did Jubilee have to do with the ministry of Jesus, spiritual and natural healing, and the grace of God? Jubilee only came once every forty-nine years.

Jubilee was the Sabbath of all sabbaths, taught in Leviticus 25. After an accumulation of the weekly Sabbaths, Saturday, comes a yearlong Sabbath, once every seven years for the land to rest from planting and growing crops. Jubilee then came after seven yearlong sabbaths, at the end of forty-nine years. Jubilee was a time for all possessions to return to the original owners, a cleansing of the national economy, to right all property violations that had occurred to individuals and families during the previous fifty years.

Jesus was telling His hometown crowd that Jubilee would no longer be a "once every fifty years" occurrence. Jesus was introducing an eternal and perpetual Jubilee.

Original Owners

"In this Year of Jubilee, each of you shall return to his possessions" (Leviticus 25:13).

After managing two businesses for a few years and pastoring a church for over thirty years, I think Jubilee must have been a legal and accounting nightmare. Imagine working for the bureau of records and being inundated by thousands of people looking for legal documents to prove original ownership for land, homes, barns, agricultural equipment, wagons, and carts for the past fifty years. It would certainly have been wise to keep personal papers of sales and purchases of possessions since the previous Jubilee. I am sure you only needed to provide a document of citizenship and all possessions could then be returned to you, the original owner.

The Swap of Goods

In proclaiming the acceptable year of the Lord, the introduction of an eternal Jubilee, Jesus was announcing what He would be doing by His death. He would return everything to its original owner. Redemption would be returned to the poor. Healing would be returned to the brokenhearted. Deliverance would be returned to the captive. Recovery of sight would be returned to the blind. And, liberty would be returned to those who were bruised. Not once every fifty years, but from then on.

This all occurred on the cross as Jesus took every curse for us of sin, poverty, and sickness.

For He [God the Father] *made Him* [Jesus Christ] *who knew no sin to be sin for us, that we might become the righteousness of God in Him* (2 Corinthians 5:21) (Author comments bracketed).

Where the first Adam sold out all of humanity and lost everything we used to possess, Jesus, the last Adam, has made provision for us to have everything returned. We are the original owners of all that was given to Adam. The Day of Atonement and a trumpet announced the beginning of Jubilee (Leviticus 25:9). So did the cross, our Day of Atonement, announce a perpetual Jubilee.

We are the original owners of all that was given to Adam.

Everything Is Returned

If someone swindled you out of an inheritance with a corrupt business deal, you received your inheritance back, and they received their corrupt deal back. Then *everything* went back to its original owner. On the cross Jesus took back our blessings, and Satan was given back all his curses. Redemption was given to us, and Satan received back his iniquity. Healing was returned to us, and Satan received back his brokenheartedness. Deliverance was returned to us, and Satan was given back his captivity. We received recovery of sight, and Satan was given back his blindness. We received our liberty, and Satan was given back his bruises. We received righteousness and every blessing attached to it. Satan was given back his sin and everything attached to it. Go to the property office of God's Word and find out what belongs to you that was taken by Satan at the fall. You can now take it back any day of the week. This is Jubilee! This is grace!

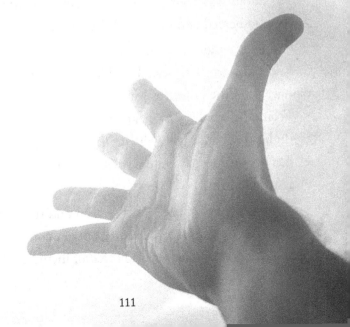

Chapter 8

The Communion Elements

God's Healing Power Is Personal to Me

Being raised in the home of a Pentecostal minister, I was taught from a very young age about divine healing. I remember as a boy a sharp pain hit me in the stomach, and I doubled over on the floor in pain. My father prayed for me in the name of Jesus and, immediately, I was healed. A few hours later, the pain hit me again, and I returned back to the floor in pain. This time, my father told Satan to turn me loose. I was already healed, but Satan was trying a counterattack to confuse us. I rose up healed and never had the pain again.

Loretta and I have also trained our own children to know and trust Jesus as their Healer as well as Savior. I have seen the power of Jesus heal both of my children. From the healing of heart trouble to fevers cooling under our hand, Jehovah Rapha, the Lord our Healer, has been a covenant name we have depended on for our family's health.

As a teacher of the Word of God and the pastor of a church, I have seen people come out of a coma, healed of minor sicknesses as well as healed of incurable diseases.

One Tough Question

But this belief has not gone unchallenged. From book pages and open confrontations, I have been challenged by other ministers that healing is not part of the atoning work of Jesus Christ even though they have found the Word of God to speak for itself, *"...Himself took our infirmities and bore our sicknesses"* (Matthew 8:17) (see also Isaiah 53:4) and *"...by His stripes we are* [and were] *healed"* (Isaiah 53:5) (Author comments bracketed) (see also 1 Peter 2:24).

I became stronger in my knowledge that forgiveness of sins and healing of the body go hand in hand. *"Who forgives all your iniquities, who heals all your diseases"* (Psalm 103:3). *"And the prayer of faith will save* [heal] *the sick, and the Lord will raise him up. And if he has committed sins, he will be forgiven"* (James 5:15) (Author comments bracketed). Jesus explained healing of sickness as an outward proof of His ability to forgive sins (Matthew 9:5-7). Divine healing is still as true today as it was in the days of the Old and New Testament.

I thought all my questions were answered and all the arguments had been explained. I thought I had heard every rebuttal until I heard a minister say, "If healing were really in the atoning work of Jesus on the cross, then whenever a person believed in Jesus as their Savior, all of their sicknesses would leave their body. Since a person can be just as sick after they are born again as before, this proves there is no healing in the atonement."

The search for the answer to this question brought me to a place I would have never suspected, the communion elements.

Three Types of Ritual for the Church Age

Unlike the Old Testament where many forms of ritual surrounded the believers of Israel, the Church has only three. Rituals, in and of themselves, have no power. Yet what they represent does have power. Church ritual today, as well as in the Old Testament, points to the work of Jesus in His redemption for us. Ritual in the Old Testament pointed forward to the work Jesus would do and ritual in the New Testament points back to the work Jesus has done.

And having spoiled principalities and powers, he made a shew of them openly, triumphing over them in it. Let no man therefore judge you in meat, or in drink, or in respect of an holyday, or of the new moon, or of the sabbath days: which are a shadow of things to come; but the body is of Christ (Colossians 2:15-17).

Three types of ritual exist for the church age. They are water baptism, anointing with oil for healing, and communion. The types of ritual given today do not point to the future, as did those under the Law, but back to the finished work of Jesus in redemption. It is also important to understand that it is never the ritual which has the power to deliver but what the ritual stands for, remembering what Jesus did for us.

Some people are convinced they should be baptized in river water. Some are even further convinced they should be baptized in the Jordan River in Israel for the ritual to truly count. But God doesn't care if you are baptized in a swimming pool or even a bathtub. It is not the place or type of water; it is what water baptism stands for that has meaning. The ritual shows that the person has already accepted Jesus Christ as their Savior.

The water symbolizes death and burial of the person's old life. Coming out of the water represents resurrection to newness of life.

Many believers are convinced the local church should use olive oil when laying hands on the sick for healing (James 5:14-15). It is true that this was probably what was used in the times of the New Testament, but God is not concerned with the type of oil. It is not the oil which heals the sick but the prayer of faith. God could not care less if you used motor oil or Crisco. The oil represents the Holy Spirit and His presence to heal.

I might also point out that the hands are not important in healing but the faith. Some people want hands laid on them by a famous minister. The hands of the individual only represent the hand of the Lord. The hand of the Lord is the divine power of the ministry of the Holy Spirit. This power will work through the hands of any believer, an evangelist, or an auto mechanic with grease on his hands (Mark 16:18).

In communion many people argue whether to have real wine or grape juice and unleavened bread or regular bread. God doesn't care if you use root beer and twinkies. Jesus said, "...*Do this in remembrance of me*"

(Luke 22:19). Keeping your attention on the finished work of the cross is what will bring the miracle power of forgiveness and divine healing. The cup and the bread are merely a point of contact for the individual to release his or her faith in the power of God. There is no merit in the element but in the remembrance.

> *For he who eats and drinks in an unworthy manner eats and drinks judgment to himself, not discerning the Lord's body. For this reason many are weak and sick among you, and many sleep* (1 Corinthians 11:29-30).

The Corinthian believers were eating the bread and drinking the cup in an unworthy manner because they were not properly understanding the meaning of the communion table. They were taking lightly the meaning of the bread and cup. The communion elements turned into a full meal and from there developed into a drunken party.

Bread and Wine

Communion speaks stronger of the grace of God than any other form of ritual we have in the Church today.

It teaches that both major works of Jesus on the cross, forgiveness of sins, and healing of sickness are products of God's grace. Both elements, the cup and the bread, are handed to the individual who is about to partake, and all the recipient does is receive them, then eat and drink. No works are involved in receiving the cup of salvation or the bread of healing. The work was done by the minister who brought them.

Communion is also different in other ways than the rituals of water baptism or anointing with oil. First, it is the only one which speaks directly of the work of Jesus on the cross for us. And, in each other form of ritual, there is only one element. Communion has two. Baptism has water, anointing uses oil, but communion uses bread and wine.

The first example of communion is given in Genesis 14:18-20 when Melchizedek, king of Salem, came out to meet Abraham after returning from the destruction of the enemy kings. Abraham returned after a great victory and his mind was momentarily not on the Lord. These elements were to remind Abraham that he did not fight and win in his own strength but in the power of God.

"And he [Melchizedek] *blessed him* [Abraham], *and said: 'Blessed be Abram of God Most High, Possessor of heaven and earth; and blessed be God Most High, who has delivered your enemies into your hand'"* (Genesis 14:19-20) (Author comments bracketed). Melchizedek, a type of Christ (the only king-priest until Jesus), gave Abraham the communion elements to put his attention back on the Lord.

This is the purpose of communion. As often as we eat and drink it, it brings us back to the place where our true life began. It helps us to remember Jesus' death and that we cannot redeem ourselves, win our own battles, or make ourselves successful without the Lord Jesus who is our life.

The two elements do not reappear again until Jesus, our King-Priest, offered them to His disciples in the upper room before His crucifixion. We are told in the New Testament to take these elements until the Lord returns. *"For as often as you eat this bread and drink this cup, you proclaim the Lord's death till He comes"* (1 Corinthians 11:26).

Each element in communion represents a different part of our redemption. The cup speaks of the shedding of Jesus' blood and the bread speaks of His broken body. The wine signifies salvation from sins, and the bread speaks of divine healing for our bodies. The inward man and the outward man were covered through Jesus' work on the cross.

Our Salvation Came through the Shed Blood of Jesus

...feed the church of God, which He has purchased with his own blood (Acts 20:28 KJV).

Much more then, having now been justified by His blood, we shall be saved from wrath through Him (Romans 5:9).

Knowing that you were not redeemed with corruptible things, like silver or gold, from your aimless conduct received by tradition from your fathers, but with the precious blood of Christ, as of a lamb without blemish and without spot (1 Peter 1:18-19).

Physical Healing Came through the Broken Body of Jesus

Surely He has borne [in His body] *our griefs* [Hebrew—sicknesses] *and carried our sorrows* [Hebrew—pains];...*and by His stripes* [Hebrew—bruises] *we are healed* (Isaiah 53:4-5) (Author comments bracketed).

Notice the reason why many of the Corinthians were weak, sick, and slept (died early): *"...not discerning the Lord's body"* (1 Corinthians 11:29-30).

When you understand and rightly discern the purpose of the bread in communion, you can receive divine healing into your body. It is possible to no longer be weak, sickly, and die prematurely. God has many promises for long life in the Word (Psalm 91:16, Ephesians 6:1-3). Here is one many have overlooked. God desires congregations to walk in divine health and live long lives without having to always call for the elders of the church.

In the church I pastored, the Sunday mornings I gave the congregation the communion elements, we did not lay hands on the sick or anoint them with oil. I taught the congregation there is healing power in the eating of the bread of communion. If they would rightly discern the power shown by the bread they held in their hands, they could be healed while they were in their seat. I have received many praise reports from people who were healed of sickness while eating the bread of communion.

Redemption is therefore twofold—as inseparably united as our inward and outward man, so is the forgiveness of sins and the healing of disease. You will never find the communion elements separated but always together.

> *Bless the Lord, O my soul; and all that is within me, bless His holy name...Who forgives all your iniquities, who heals all your diseases* (Psalm 103:1,3).

> *And the prayer of faith will save* [heal] *the sick, and the Lord will raise him up. And if he has committed sins, he will be forgiven* (James 5:15) (Author comments bracketed).

Jesus showed the religious men of His day that healing for the body was as easy to accomplish as the forgiveness of sins. Jesus even went on to state that the healing of the body was the outward manifestation of His ability to forgive sins.

> *For which is easier, to say, "Your sins are forgiven you," or to say, "Arise and walk"? But that you may know that the Son of Man has power on earth to forgive sins—then He said to the paralytic, "Arise, take up your bed, and go to your house" (Matthew 9:5-6).*

The Greek word for *save* (*sozo*) is also translated "healed" in Mark 5:23 and Luke 8:36 and "whole" in Mark 5:28, 34. The same word for *salvation* is used for the healing of the body. The two works are inseparably tied together by the redemption of Jesus on the cross.

Simple Faith

Faith is the means of receiving both salvation and divine healing. Faith receives the forgiveness of God and the healing power accomplished for us on the cross. We drink the wine and eat the bread. Eating and drinking are both types of faith in the Word of God.

> *Ho! Everyone who thirsts, come to the water, and you who have no money, come, buy and eat. Yes, come, buy wine and milk without money and without price* (Isaiah 55:1).
>
> *I am the bread of life...This is the bread which comes down from heaven, that one may eat of it and not die* (John 6:48,50).
>
> *On the last day, that great day of the feast, Jesus stood and cried out, saying, "If anyone thirsts, let him come to Me and drink"* (John 7:37).

Eating and drinking are something anyone can do. You do not have to be educated, male or female, or high in society to eat and drink. Moral, immoral, fat, skinny, educated, uneducated, black, white, handsome, ugly, male or female, all can drink and eat. Faith is always compared to something anyone can do because salvation, healing, or any of God's gifts are for whosoever will. My favorite example of faith in the Word is opening the eyes.

Look to Me, and be saved, all you ends of the earth! For I am God, and there is no other (Isaiah 45:22).

When the children of Israel were bitten by fiery serpents in the camp, God gave the command for the healing of the people. *"Then the Lord said to Moses, 'Make a fiery serpent, and set it on a pole; and it shall be that everyone who is bitten, when he looks at it, shall live'"* (Numbers 21:8). A person can be as tired as possible and have no strength left in his body to lift a finger, but he can still open his eyes. The eyelids require the least amount of strength in the body. This is all the strength required to receive from the hand of God. Many of us have heard of people who were paralyzed in their whole body and the only way they could communicate with those around them was through the blinking of their eyes. Look and live!

A Simple Solution

We now return to our first question for which this chapter was written. "If Jesus atoned for our sicknesses as well as our sins on the cross, why are we not healed of our diseases when we accept Jesus as our Savior?"

The solution is simple. The two elements in communion are taken separately.

> *For I received from the Lord that which I also delivered to you: that the Lord Jesus on the same night in which He was betrayed took bread; and when He had given thanks, He broke it and said, "Take, eat; this is My body which is broken for you; do this in remembrance of Me." In the same manner He also took the cup after supper, saying, "This cup is the new covenant in My blood. This do, as often as you drink it, in remembrance of Me." For as often as you eat this bread and drink this cup, you proclaim the Lord's death till He comes. But let a man examine himself, and so let him eat of the bread and drink of the cup* (1 Corinthians 11:23-26,28).

Although the communion elements are served together, they are not received together. Jesus' blood and body went to the cross together, but the elements are taken one after the other, the bread and then the cup.

When I received Jesus as my Savior, my diseases were not healed because I partook of the cup, not the bread. Divine healing is something I learned about and received later. Both are received by faith but not at the same time. The two elements do not have the same purpose nor are taken at the same time, even if only seconds separate eating the bread and drinking of the cup.

When this truth dawned on me, I made a new declaration of faith. I received Jesus as my personal Healer, just as I had received Him as my personal Savior. I ate the bread just as I had drunk of the cup. I have led the congregation in a confession that Jesus is now the Deliverer of their bodies just as He is the Savior of their souls. Now they can learn to resist symptoms of sickness and disease just as they have learned to resist the temptations of sin.

Drink from the Cup of Salvation

I invite you to join with me in partaking of spiritual communion. If you have never received Jesus Christ as your Lord and Savior, I invite you to pray this prayer and drink of the cup.

"Father, I believe in my heart that you raised Jesus from the dead just for me. I also confess with my mouth that Jesus is now my Lord and Savior, and I am no longer under the control of Satan, the prince of this world. I am now Your very own child. Old things are passed away and all things are become new. I also know now I will spend eternity in heaven with You. I have passed from death into true life. I thank You for the gift of the blood of Your Son Jesus Christ. Amen"

Eat the Bread of Healing

If you have never received Jesus Christ as your personal Healer, I invite you to pray this prayer and eat of the bread.

"Father, I believe that Jesus Himself took my infirmities and bore my sicknesses. I believe that with the stripes He took in His body, I am now healed. I receive Jesus as my personal Healer just as I have received Him as my Lord and Savior. Your power to resist sickness is inside of me. I thank You for the gift of the body of Your Son Jesus Christ. I thank You for Your grace. Amen."

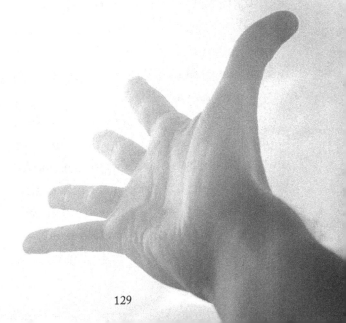

Chapter 9

Compassion and Healing

Imitators of God

Therefore be imitators of God as dear children. And walk in love, as Christ also has loved us and given Himself for us, an offering and a sacrifice to God for a sweet-smelling aroma (Ephesians 5:1-2).

Paul warns the Corinthian ministers not to imitate other ministers or strive to reach their standards. He said to compare yourselves with others is *"...not wise"* (2 Corinthians 10:12). We can learn from others, just don't try to be them. The levels of other people are not the goals we shoot to reach.

But we are to imitate someone: God. Our passage in Ephesians tell us we are to imitate God. The Greek word for *imitate* is *mimites*, where we get our English word *mimic*. We are also to imitate the walk of Jesus in our daily life on earth. The main message here is to imitate God who is love and imitate the love walk of Jesus. Love and compassion for others should be our main goal. Jesus was not moved by anger, self-gratification, or receiving appreciation from others, but to put the needs of others above Himself. This is the true walk of love we are to imitate.

Can Anger and Compassion Coexist?

The answer to this question is an emphatic "yes." What and who you are angry with and who you have compassion for are the bottom line. We can be *"...angry, and sin not..."* (Ephesians 4:26 KJV). Part of the love walk includes knowing when and who to be angry at, and when and for whom to show compassion.

Anger is to be shown toward Satan and his works. Jesus became angry toward the turning of the temple into a business selling sacrificial animals. He threw out the moneychangers and beat with a whip those making money. Jesus spent an entire chapter dealing with the teachings and religious hypocrisy of the scribes and Pharisees in Matthew 23. He said they *"...devour widow's houses..."* (vs.14), *"...you travel land and sea to win one proselyte, and when he is won, you make him twice as much a son of hell as yourselves"* (vs.15). He called them *"'whitewashed tombs which indeed appear beautiful outwardly, but inside are full of dead men's bones and all uncleanness"* (vs.27). It is obvious Jesus hated the teaching and practice of lies lived by the Pharisees, yet He went two days later to the cross and died for them. He also died for the false teachers we have today (2 Peter 2:1).

Jesus hated the teaching and practice of sin, but He loved the people who were teaching and committing the sin, enough to die for them. Jesus went everywhere healing *"...all who were oppressed by the devil..."* (Acts 10:38). He apparently hated the works of Satan but loved the people caught in them. God was so pleased with Jesus and His finished work on earth that He commended Jesus before He sat down at His right hand, saying, *"You have loved righteousness and hated lawlessness"* (Hebrews 1:9).

We see this in society among those in the medical field. We love healing and hate disease. Healing is our friend, and sickness is an enemy. We treat breast cancer, heart disease, and diabetes as enemies and seek to conquer them. We want to make them history like many other diseases we have seen abolished by the medical profession through the years. Love and compassion toward people should be the driving force for us to rid them of the sin, sickness, and works of the devil we hate.

How often do we use our spiritual weapons against each other? They were meant to be used against Satan. We do not have authority over people but over demons and the works of Satan. Our God-given gifts and authority are not spiritual witchcraft to get people to do what we want them to do. Even God cannot make people get saved or force them to serve Him. Compassion is used to meet people's needs, so they will want to serve this God of grace and mercy.

Compassion Drove the Ministry of Jesus

When Jesus went out He saw a great multitude; and He was moved with compassion toward them, and healed their sick (Matthew 14:14).

Like Jesus, our compassion for people is what should back our God given-authority over Satan and his works. How Jesus looks at both sickness and people should be how we also look at them. Jesus called a woman He healed in the temple a "daughter of Abraham," but of her sickness, He said, "...*Satan has bound...*" her (Luke 13:16). Compassion loves people and seeks to rid them of the works of Satan that bind them.

Compassion Drives the Grace of God

> *The Lord is gracious and full of compassion,*
> *slow to anger and great in mercy. The Lord is*
> *good to all, and His tender mercies are over all*
> *His works* (Psalm 145:8-9).

Whether it is the forgiveness of sins, meeting our spiritual and temporal needs, or healing our diseases, God's compassion and His great mercies are behind all His works. To have compassion is to love abundantly, show mercy, and greatly desire to help someone else. Compassion is a good synonym for grace. It looks to receive back nothing but to bless the one who is in need only. It is not given *"grudgingly or of necessity"* (2 Corinthians 9:7) but only to rejoice in the finished deed of blessing another. Compassion is the reason behind God's grace.

Compassion is not what God can do, but what He earnestly desires to do. Jesus immediately answered the leper who asked if He was willing to heal him with "I will!" Eager compassion answers "Yes!" even before the question "Will you?" leaves the mouth. In fact, God's compassion helps us to understand why every need we can have has already been planned for and met from before the foundation of the world. And God is continually searching for an opportunity to forgive, bless, and heal anyone who will call on Him.

Compassion is a good synonym for grace.

For the eyes of the Lord run to and fro throughout the whole earth, to shew Himself strong on behalf of those whose heart is perfect toward Him (2 Chronicles 16:9 KJV).

Our Lord "*delights in mercy*" (Micah 7:18).

The "*mercy of the Lord is from everlasting to everlasting*" (Psalm 103:17).

There is no God in heaven or on earth like You, who keep Your covenant and mercy with Your servants who walk before You with all their hearts (2 Chronicles 6:14).

Mercy Is the Cry of Our Hearts

God responds to a cry for mercy and then acts in mercy, grace for grace. Two blind men sat beside the road and heard Jesus was close by. They both cried out, "Have mercy on us." Jesus heard them and *"had compassion on them and touched their eyes. And immediately their eyes received sight..."* (Matthew 20:29-34).

Seeking God's grace is what brings us the answers we have been looking for all along. Forgiveness of sins does not come because we approach God with our religious works and kind deeds to others. Remission comes when we reach out with our faith to receive what God only can supply. So it is with the healing of our disease. God does not heal us because of our good works or pleasing personality. He heals us when we reach out in faith to receive the finished work of healing Jesus accomplished on the cross. *"...Daughter, your faith has made you well"* (Mark 5:34).

What Can I Do for You?

The religious men of Jesus' day put great stipulations on forgiveness of sins and healing of diseases. Much argument was made against Jesus for forgiving sin or healing people on the Sabbath. The fact that Jesus healed Gentiles, forgave adultery, and declared a man's sins to be forgiven, brought wrath from the religious crowd. Jesus finally shut the mouths of the legalistic Pharisees by asking, *"Which is easier, to say, 'Your sins are forgiven,' or to say, 'Arise and walk'"?* (Matthew 9:5). For Jesus one was as easy as the other. For the religious crowd, both were impossible.

Religion seeks people without needs and asks, "What can you do for me?" Jesus continually sought out the needy and asked, "What can I do for you?" This is the voice of compassion and mercy. This is the voice of grace. *"But go and learn what this means: 'I desire mercy and not sacrifice.' For I did not come to call the righteous, but sinners, to repentance"* (Matthew 9:13).

We could add to this verse "and the sick to be healed." Jesus is not looking for our good deeds, lists of accomplishments, and praise from others we have helped. He is looking for sinners who will admit they have sinned and the sick to admit they are sick. Jesus is looking for those who are looking for the grace of God in forgiveness and in healing.

Why don't you just become honest with God and cry out for His mercy. Have you committed sins? He is faithful and just to forgive you if you will just confess the sin and admit you have failed. Are you in need of healing? Cry out to God for Him to have mercy on you. A cry for mercy will be met with mercy. You cannot heal yourself any more than you can save yourself or forgive you own sins. Trust God, and He will abundantly pardon and completely heal.

Chapter 10

Back to Adam

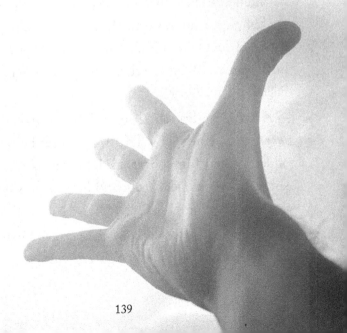

Daily Grace

Grace, like most every other work of God in our life, does not end at salvation. Grace continues past the new birth and becomes woven into the fabric of our daily life, spiritual and natural. Although we are now citizens of heaven (Philippians 3:20), we are also still, temporarily, citizens of this earth. My momentary home is in Oklahoma, but my eternal home is in heaven, waiting for my entrance. In essence, I have a dual citizenship. My greater allegiance is to my eternal home, heaven, and my secondary allegiance is to my temporary home on earth. There are *two me's:* spiritual Bob and natural Bob. I have this treasure, the new birth, in an earthen vessel, my body. Spiritual Bob lives inside of natural Bob.

After my salvation, a new phase of grace began— *more grace* (James 4:6). There will never be a need for added grace to my salvation. Jesus did not forget one sin or overlook one disease and have to go back to the cross and die for it.

I do not increase or grow in the new birth. But in my daily life after salvation, I am constantly in need of more grace for growth. In heaven, I am seated. The work is done. But, in my daily life I am standing or walking, ever resisting Satan and the world, and moving toward new destinations. What I know to be true in the new creation needs to be brought over and applied to my everyday walk with Jesus. In other words, the Word I learn in church on Sunday needs to be put to use on Monday, making tuna fish sandwiches for my children's lunch or putting up with daily work at the office. Living a life and a witness for Jesus before the world requires *more grace* because what I know in theory must be taken to the lab class of life.

Two You's

Today, there are different terms found in our Bible and definitions used by ministers of the Word to define our spiritual and natural life. Some of them are as follows:

Positional and Temporal Truth.

Paul divided his epistles into two major divisions, teaching us who we are "in Christ" in the opening chapters and then switching over to application of those truths to our daily lives. We, who were told we were the righteousness of God in the opening chapters of Ephesians, are now told not to lie or disrespect authority but honor our husbands, love our wives, and raise godly children.

Relationship and fellowship.

Similar to our natural family relationships, God tells us that as His children, we were born into a relationship that cannot be taken away. But our fellowship, as with our own children, can change not only daily, but often from minute to minute. The forgiveness of sins which brought us into relationship will never be dealt with again. But the sins of daily life are in constant need of forgiveness. When I was saved, God made me a member of the royal priesthood. As a priest I can now approach my High Priest, Jesus, and confess my daily sins and get immediate and full cleansing of them. These sins do not separate me from my relationship with God, but with my daily fellowship, communion, joy, and peace with the Father.

Bathing and foot washing.

Jesus used this example with Peter who, as a believer, thought he needed to be washed all over again when he sinned. Jesus told him that whoever has been bathed only needed to have his feet washed (John 13:10). We were bathed completely, had our sins forgiven at the new birth, and those sins will never be dealt with again. But our feet walk through this world, and dust and daily sins accumulate on them. We need to wash our feet with the confession of these daily sins. A tub full of water is needed for a bath, but only a small laver is needed to wash our feet—a lot of water and a little water.

Shedding and sprinkling of blood.

Just as the children of Israel were about to cross the Red Sea, they had to kill and eat the Passover lamb. The shed blood of the lamb was drained into a bowl, and then a small amount was sprinkled over and around the entry, the doorpost. The blood shed into the bowl represented Jesus' blood for the remission of our sins. We are now protected from the wrath of God in time and eternity. But the blood sprinkled over and around the door was to keep out Satan, the "destroyer," from entering the house (Exodus 12:23, 1 Corinthians 10:10). It took a whole bowl of blood to redeem us and make us a part of God's family. But it only takes a few drops around the door into our life to keep Satan out and from robbing, killing, and destroying us with sin, sickness, and the temptations of sin.

Spirit cleansing and conscience cleansing.

Our spirits were made clean at the new birth and will never need to be made clean again. But the cleansing of our souls, or our consciences, must be handled each time we sin and are then tempted to overlook the confessing of the sin. Our spirits were made righteous by the blood Jesus shed, but our consciences are made clear and clean by the blood being sprinkled (Hebrews 10:22).

When you were saved, your spirit was made righteous and will never have to be made righteous again. Your personal sins never enter your spirit. They enter your soul or your thoughts, and they have to be purged. The same blood that cleansed your spirit once now cleanses your soul frequently. It just takes a lot less of the blood for daily cleansing than it took for your eternal salvation.

Done and Being Done

What I need in daily life has already been accomplished in my spiritual life. I can be forgiven for daily sins because I have already been forgiven of my sins at the new birth. I have it in my new man, my spirit, but need it in my old man, my body. It may sound a little confusing but let me put it this way: I can live as a Christian because I am a Christian. But I had to become a Christian before I could act as one. Christians are not supposed to sin, but they do. I do not always listen to the real Bob, the new man; I sometimes listen and obey the temporary Bob, the old man. But since I have the new man, I can conquer the old man. The power given at the new birth provides me power to overcome the failings of the first birth.

Again, the sins I commit in my daily life do not remove my salvation; they temporarily remove my fellowship with God. When I ask for forgiveness, I am asking as a Christian, not a sinner. My daily forgiveness that is received does not reinstate me into heaven; it reinstates my position of power against my flesh and Satan. Satan, who got into the door, now has to retreat back outside. I am either a spiritual Christian, under the control of the Holy Spirit, or a carnal Christian, under the control of my flesh (1 Corinthians 3:1-3). In either case, I am a Christian. I can get forgiven of daily sins in my natural life because I have already been forgiven of all sins in my spiritual life. I am only taking what is present in my spirit and bringing it over to be used in my natural life. Whatever natural Bob needs is already present in spiritual Bob.

The grace of healing is the same. I am already healed in my born-again, recreated spirit. I am transferring it over into my physical body where it is needed. Like daily sanctification, healing is simply received by faith in God's promises.

The Parting of the Red Sea

...Moses stretched out his hand over the sea; and the Lord caused the sea to go back by a strong east wind all that night, and made the sea dry land, and the waters were divided. So the children of Israel went into the midst of the sea on dry ground, and the waters were a wall to them on the right hand and on their left (Exodus 14:21-22).

Let's look at a few points concerning this incredible miracle.

First, the parting of the Red Sea was preceded by the Passover. The Passover represented the work of Jesus, the Lamb of God, for us on the cross. The lamb was slain, its blood removed, and then it was roasted over fire, a type of judgement. The lamb was innocent; the people of Israel were not. Jesus was innocent yet died in our place; the innocent died for the guilty.

Second, what happened at the Red Sea is a type of salvation. It was impossible for Israel to do anything except obey the word of Moses, "...*Do not be afraid. Stand still, and see the salvation of the Lord...*" (Exodus 14:13). So it is with our salvation. All we can do is stand and watch the work of Jesus for us. God did all the work. We, as Israel, do nothing. This is grace.

Third, the waters that parted and allowed Israel to cross, also came back together and destroyed Israel's enemies permanently. The same water that delivered a blessing to Israel was a curse to Egypt's strength. The same blood that set us free also spoiled Satan's army of principalities and powers and made an open show of them (Colossians 2:15).

Fourth, Egypt was a type of our life before Jesus delivered us. We were in slavery to Satan and sin (Romans 6:17, 20) and now have been set free.

Fifth, the wilderness Israel was delivered into was not their ultimate promised goal. That was Canaan. The wilderness is a type of the life of growth we all must pass through to be mature enough to handle the blessings and abundance God has for us when we reach discipleship, which is Canaan. The wilderness is a place where we are tested to put the Word of God above what we see, hear, or experience.

Sixth, the waters of the Red Sea divided in two different directions. Jesus judged and conquered our sins past, present, and future. We stand in the present, in the middle. As we look back, no sin can ever erase what Jesus did for us at the cross or the new birth. As we look straight ahead to the present, then forward to the future, we know that nothing present or anything to come can separate us from the love of God and His greatest gift of that love, which is eternal life.

The Jordan River

Forty years later, the second generation, under the leadership of Caleb and Joshua, came to the borders of Canaan, the Jordan River. Another body of water stood between them and their inheritance.

...Those who bore the ark came to the Jordan, and the feet of the priests who bore the ark dipped in the edge of the water (for the Jordan overflows all its banks during the whole time of harvest), that the waters which came down from upstream stood still, and rose in a heap very far away at Adam, the city that is beside Zaretan. So the waters that went down into the Sea of the Arabah, the Salt Sea, failed, and were cut off; and the people crossed over opposite Jericho (Joshua 3:15-16).

Let's take a look at some of the points concerning this incredible miracle as Israel came to the end of forty years in the wilderness and crossed over Jordan to take possession of their Promised Land.

First, the Jordan represents forgiveness of sins for a Christian, not salvation for an unbeliever. This body of water, a river, was nowhere near the size of the Red Sea. Since the Jordan was at flood stage, it too was impossible to cross, even though it was a smaller body of water. We are no more capable of forgiving our own daily sins as we were to redeem ourselves as a sinner.

Second, no sacrifice was needed before crossing. The priests were the first to step in. When the soles of their shoes touched the edge of the water, the water backed up and Israel went over. We as priests no longer need to sacrifice Jesus again. He died one time. From now on, we confess our sins, and the daily transgressions we face back up and let us cross over. The Red Sea was a one-way journey. No one went back. But, two tribes decided to remain on the entry side of Jordan and did not possess the land with the rest of the tribes. You can stay in carnality if you want, but you are cut off from the blessings God has for you. Simply confess your sins and walk ahead to the abundance of Canaan, the overcoming Christian life.

The Red Sea was a one-way journey.

Third, the waters of the Jordan backed up in only one direction. Your daily sins can be forgiven and nothing you have ever committed in life can hold you back. You can look back from where you stand today and realize that Satan cannot hold it over your head for the sins you committed yesterday, last week, last year, or decades ago. On the other hand, you cannot receive forgiveness today for a sin you will commit tomorrow. The waters back up in one direction—toward the past. There is no such thing as confessing your upcoming sins. "God forgive me for what I am about to do" is a useless prayer.

Fourth, the waters of the Jordan backed up to a city named Adam. There is no sin in your family or family tree that can stop you today. When you confess your sins, God holds nothing against you all the way back to Adam. There is no such thing as a family or generational curse if you have a conscience free from sin. Every family can be traced back to Adam, and he, nor any of his descendants, hold anything over you. When you confess your sins, God is faithful and just to forgive you of that sin and then cleanse you from *all* unrighteousness. This means if you confess the sin you know of, He is even faithful to forgive you of the ones you *don't* know of. You are clean not only in your spirit, but also in your soul and daily life. It is just as much grace in your daily forgiveness as a Christian as it was in your salvation. You could not redeem yourself and become saved, and you cannot forgive yourself and become a spiritual believer. It may take less blood, just a sprinkle, or less water, a river and not a sea, but both are impossible for you to accomplish. You needed God's grace as a sinner to be saved from your sins, and you still need God's grace as a Christian to be forgiven from your daily sins after you are saved.

The Grace of Healing

Just as you were forgiven of all sins when you received Jesus, so you can be when you confess your daily sins as a Christian. I can *be* forgiven because I *am* forgiven. My natural life then lines up with my spiritual life.

So it is with healing. The children of Israel left Egypt and crossed the Red Sea, not only already forgiven but already healed.

> *He also brought them out also with silver and gold, and there was none feeble among His tribes* (Psalm 105:37).

If we were to see into our spirits, we would not only see that we have been forgiven back to Adam but also we have been healed back to Adam. Faith takes the truth that is in our recreated, born-again spirits and makes it a reality in our natural lives. Whether it is righteousness or healing, we received it all when we were saved. Faith transfers it to our natural body. If no sin back to Adam can stop me, there are no generational curses of sin that might have occurred in my family tree in the past that can stop me today.

So it is with healing. There is no generational curse of cancer, diabetes, or depression that can hinder me today. I don't need to curse any sin, witchcraft, sickness, or disease in my past or in my ancestors. Jesus did it for me on the cross. All I need to make sure of is that no sin is present in my life. If there is sin, I simply confess it, and I am eligible to transfer the healing Jesus gave me at my salvation and bring it over into my body. I can declare "there is no feebleness in me." If I confess my faults to God or anyone I have sinned against, I will be healed (James 5:16).

This is your righteousness. This is your healing. This is God's grace.

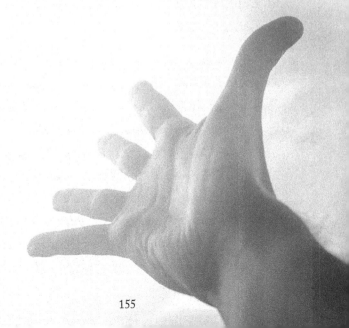

Salvation by Grace through Faith

Salvation is a gift of God for you! He's provided salvation for you by His grace, and you receive it through your simple faith!

No matter who you are and no matter your past, God loves you so much that He gave His one and only begotten Son for you. The Bible says, *"…Whoever believes in Him shall not perish but have eternal life"* (John 3:16 NASB). Jesus laid down His life and rose again so you could spend eternity with Him and experience His absolute best on earth.

If you would like to receive Jesus as your Savior and Lord, pray the following prayer out loud from your heart.

> *Heavenly Father, I come to you admitting that I am a sinner. Right now, I choose to turn away from sin, and I ask you to cleanse me of all unrighteousness. I believe that Your Son, Jesus, died on the cross to take away my sins. I also believe that He rose again from the dead so that I might be forgiven of my sins and made righteous through faith in Him. I call upon the name of Jesus Christ to be the Savior and Lord of my life. Jesus, I choose*

to follow You and ask that You fill me with the power of the Holy Spirit. I declare that right now I am a child of God. I am free from sin and full of the righteousness of God. I am saved in Jesus' name. Amen.

If you prayed this prayer to receive Jesus Christ as your Savior for the first time, please write to us with the good news! We'll send you a free book to encourage you in your new life in Him!

Harrison House Publishers
P.O. Box 310
Shippensburg, PA 17257-0310

OTHER BOOKS BY BOB YANDIAN

Calling and Separation
Decently and in Order
Faith's Destination
From Just Enough to Overflowing
God's Word to Pastors
How Deep Are the Stripes?
Leadership Secrets of David the King
Let God's Will Find You
Life & Power
Morning Moments
One Flesh
Proverbs
Rising Out of the Pit
The Bible and National Defense
The Grace of Healing
Understanding End Times
Unlimited Partnership
What If the Best Is Yet to Come?
When God is Silent

A New Testament Commentary Series
(sold individually or as a set):

Acts
Colossians
Ephesians
Galatians
Hebrews
James
Philippians
Romans

About Bob Yandian

BOB YANDIAN pastored Grace Church in Tulsa, Oklahoma for 33 years. In 2013, he began a new phase of ministry and passed the pastoral baton to his son, Robb. Bob's mission is to train up a new generation in the Word of God through his "Student of the Word" broadcast and by ministering at Bible schools, ministers' conferences, and churches. Bob is a graduate of Trinity Bible College and has served as instructor and Dean of Instructors at RHEMA Bible Training Center. Called a "pastor's pastor," Bob established the School of the Local Church that has trained and sent hundreds of ministers to churches and missions organizations around the world.

The Harrison House Vision

Proclaiming the truth and the power

of the Gospel of Jesus Christ with excellence.

Challenging Christians

to live victoriously,

grow spiritually,

know God intimately.

Connect with us on

f Facebook @ HarrisonHousePublishers

and **⬡** Instagram @ HarrisonHousePublishing

so you can stay up to date with news

about our books and our authors.

Visit us at **www.harrisonhouse.com**

for a complete product listing as well as

monthly specials for wholesale distribution.